Turntable Technique

The Art of the DJ

By Stephen Webber

Berklee Press

Director: Dave Kusek
Managing Editor: Debbie Cavalier
Marketing Manager: Ola Frank
Senior Writer/Editor: Jonathan Feist
Writer/Editor: Susan Gedutis
Contributing Editor: David Franz
Product Manager: Ilene Altman

1140 Boylston Street
Boston, MA 02215-3693 USA

Visit Berklee Press Online at
www.berkleepress.com

Contents

Part 1. Playing the Turntables

Part 2. Interviews

Acknowledgements

Special thanks to:

Dave Kusek for his vision and friendship.

Debbie Cavalier for being a consummate professional.

Jonathan Feist and Susan Gedutis for their hard work getting the thing finally completed.

Christie Z-Pabon of the DMC and Tools of War for providing guidance and historical perspective.

Tiffany Deang with the ISP for her professionalism and enthusiasm.

Composer/percussionist Jeanine Cowan for invaluable help with the musical transcriptions.

James Nixon for transcribing the interviews.

I'm especially thankful to all of the Berklee DJs who provided direct input:

DJ Edan (aka Edan Portnoy), Syndrome (aka Ken Dziok), DJ Soothe (aka Stacy Briscoe), DJ Devious (aka Dave Kramer), and DJ Reazon (aka Geoff Abramczyk).

And to QBert, Swamp, MixMaster Mike, A-Trak, Craze, and Kuttin Kandi for their great insights.

All of my friends, colleagues, students, and alumni from Berklee College of Music, especially Pat Pattison, Jeff Dorenfeld, Bill Scheniman, Rob Jaczko, David Mash, Gary Burton, Lee and Susan Berk, Watson Reid, Mitch Benoff, Carl Beatty, Mark Wessel, Terry Becker, Wayne Wadhams, Richard Mendelson, Don Puluse, Dan Thompson, Ivan Sever, Phil Levy, Wil Sandals, Andrew Martin, Ted Speaker, Bob Horn, Jonathan Gorman, Jeff Rothschild, Casey Driessen, Anne Chandler, and Chad Seay.

To my parents and sister, thanks for putting writing in the family.

Much love to Susan, Aubrey, and Angela. Thanks for being patient through my constant absence during this project.

Dedicated to the memory of Chris Yeoman.

PART 1.

Playing the Turntables

Turntable Technique: The Record!

TRACK LIST

Side One

1) ONE!
        (110.4 bpm funk jam)

2) Techno Miles
        (110.4 bpm techno-funk groove)

3) Savage Skratch Substance
        (Outrageous sound effects, sound design, spoken word)

4) Hot White Noise
        (Perfect for scratching)

5) MassAve Tone
        (Huge bass tone for fader techniques and scratching)

Side Two

1) Exercises 1–6
        (Basic scratch)

2) Exercises 7–13
        (Basic scratch with syncopation)

3) Exercise 14
        (Fills)

4) Exercises 15–21
        (Fader work out)

5) Exercises 22–26
        (Stab)

6) Exercises 27–34
        (Scratching with continuous eighth notes)

7) Exercises 35–38
        (Cutting with "one"!)

8) Exercises 39–45
        (Crossfader)

9) Exercises 46–49
        (2-hands with x-fader)

10) Exercises 50–57
        (Crab)

11) Exercise 58
        (*William Tell Skratchature*)

1. Introduction

Playing the turntable as a musical instrument is a lot of fun, and it's pretty easy to get started. You can take the study of DJing and playing the turntable as far as your imagination, discipline, and desire lead you.

Fig. 1.1. Playing the turntable

This book is meant to serve as:

1. a starting place for learning the basics of scratching and playing the turntable as a musical instrument

2. a resource for DJs to learn more about musical terms and techniques

3. a reference containing insights from top DJs and a brief history of the art form

What Kind of Instrument is This, Anyway?

The turntable can be approached as a musical instrument of amazing depth and versatility. It is very effective as a percussion instrument, capable of producing precise and complex rhythmic figures for solos, or inventive fills between vocal and instrumental lines.

Combined with a mixer, a turntable can also be used as an analog sampler. It can play spoken words and musical phrases, forward or backward, at any speed, pitch, or volume.

With two turntables, you can morph beats into different time signatures and tempos on the spot. You can cut and paste sounds seamlessly in real time, in front of an audience.

The turntable/mixer setup is also similar to a synthesizer. You can control the attack, decay, sustain, and release (ADSR) of any tone in real time using the mixer's faders.

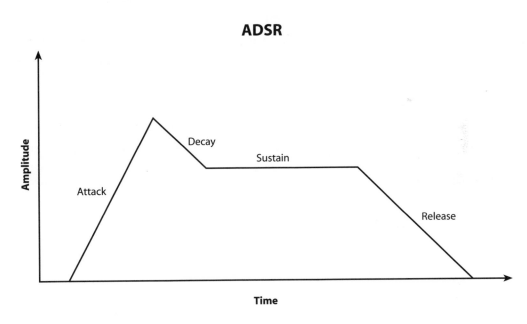

Fig. 1.2. ADSR synthesis chart

The turntable can be a melodic instrument, too. Using records with sustained tones, you can play melodies by manipulating the pitch slider and the 33-1/3 and 45 speed buttons. You can glide in and out of notes, and achieve musical effects such as vibrato and tremolo. The *Vital Vinyl* records are a great source of sustained tones for this technique.

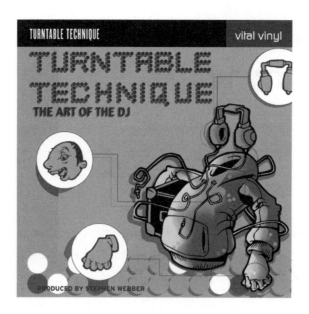

Fig. 1.3. *Turntable Technique* record jacket

Like a synthesizer or sampler, the turntable can be transformed into thousands of different instruments, just by changing records. But unlike many digital machines, playing the turntable is a physical experience, more like pulling a bow across a cello string than pushing a button or clicking a mouse.

If using the turntable as a musical instrument still seems farfetched, consider that the bow itself started out as a weapon for prehistoric humans, and developed into a sophisticated device for making music. It seems less of a leap to consider that the turntable (a device invented to play music) could evolve into an expressive instrument.

BEYOND THE TURNTABLE...

The ability of a DJ to captivate a dance floor with their knowledge of records, musicianship, and ability to read the crowd are crucial aspects of the DJ tradition.

Continued innovations, such as more extensive pitch controls, will help the turntable reach its full potential. But the turntable has already been adapted by imaginative musicians to create new musical forms capable of conveying emotion from one human being to another. And that is the true test of any instrument.

2. Equipment

The Basic Setup

The basic turntable DJ setup is made up of:

- two turntables (with cartridges and slip mats)

- a DJ mixer

You'll need an amplified stereo playback system to hear what you're doing. Headphones will come in handy for cueing up records.

Just add records and mix...

Headphones

Left Turntable

DJ Mixer

Right Turntable

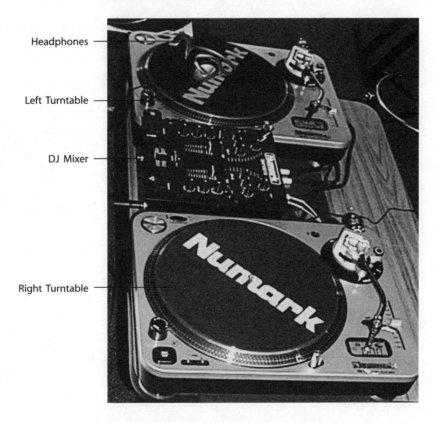

Fig. 2.1. A basic turntable DJ setup

It's important that you set up your equipment on a very sturdy surface. You don't want your equipment to shift from side to side while you are scratching.

Set up your turntables and mixer at the same height. A little above the waist seems the preferred level for most DJs. Experiment to find the most comfortable height for you.

Turntables

There are many excellent turntables on the market today. The high-end models tend to be heavy, precision instruments that absorb shock and avoid skips.

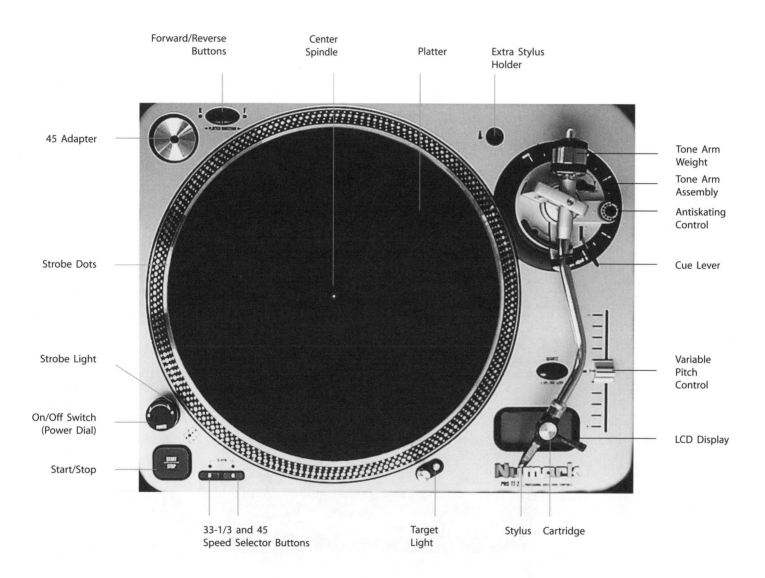

Fig. 2.2. Turntable

With few variations, DJ turntables all have the following components:

On/Off Switch (Power Dial)

Provides power to the turntable's stylus, but does not spin the platter. There are scratching techniques, such as the "basic (or baby) scratch," that will take advantage of this separation.

Start/Stop Button

Engages (or disengages) the turntable's motor, causing the platter to spin (or to stop spinning). Pressing this button while the record is playing gives a "grinding to a halt" effect, which can be put to good use. There are modifications that allow the turntable to spin backwards by double clicking on this control. The turntable pictured features separate forward/reverse buttons.

33-1/3 and 45 Speed Selector Buttons

Control the speed the platter spins, measured in "revolutions per minute" (rpm). At 33-1/3 rpm, a record completes 33 and 1/3 rotations in one minute.

Variable Pitch Control

Changes the speed of a record, which also changes the pitch. Most DJ turntables have a single sliding Variable Pitch control for both 33-1/3 rpm and 45 rpm settings. Some have two sliders: one for 33-1/3 rpm and another for 45 rpm.

These controls come in handy while beat matching. By altering the speed of a new record (while listening in the headphones), you can match the tempo of the record that is already playing on the other turntable.

Variable pitch controls and 33/45 switches can also be used to play melodies by playing a record of a constant tone. The *Vital Vinyl* series contains tones designed specifically for playing melodies on the turntable.

Cue Lever

Lifts and lowers the tone arm. Not many professional DJs use the cue lever all that much. I recommend that you get comfortable lifting the tone arm by hand and placing it accurately on the record.

Cartridge

Houses the stylus. Many cartridges mount into the head-shell assembly with two screws. Four color-coded wires connect to terminals of the same color. When you install a cartridge, be sure to follow the installation instructions carefully. There are several sturdy cartridges available for scratch DJs. Some come with their own head-shell assembly. The head-shell assembly mounts in the tone-arm tube lock and is held in place by turning the lock ring clockwise (when viewed from the rear).

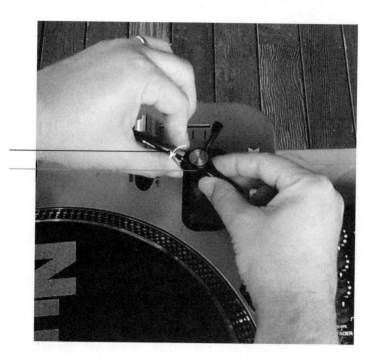

Tone Arm
Tube Lock

Head-shell
Assembly

Fig. 2.3. Mounting the head-shell assembly

Stylus

Includes the needle, which makes direct contact with the records. The stylus mounts onto the cartridge. A new stylus usually ships with a needle protector; you'll obviously need to remove this before playing records. How often you replace your stylus depends on wear. Contributing factors include the amount of weight you use, your individual scratching style, and how well everything is aligned.

Tone Arm

Supports the stylus and carries the connections (wires) from the stylus to the turntable. At the back end of the tone arm are the weights; at the front end, the cartridge. Many DJs set up the turntable so that the tone arm is across the top, out of the way.

Tone Arm Weight

Regulates the pressure on the stylus. Generally, the more weight on the tone arm, the more pressure on the needle to stay in the grooves, which can minimize skipping. However, more weight can wear out records faster and cause "burning" (saturating records with white noise). Another possible downside to more weight is increased needle wear.

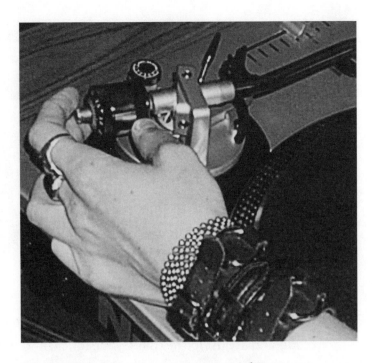

Fig. 2.4. Adjusting the tone-arm weight

To increase the amount of weight on the tone arm, rotate the weight so that it moves towards the stylus end of the tone arm.

Fig. 2.5. The tone-arm weight mounted backwards

Tone-Arm Height Adjustment

Changes the angle of the stylus in the groove. Some DJs prefer to raise the tone arm to angle the stylus down in the groove. To adjust the height of the tone arm on many DJ turntables, grip the base of the tone-arm assembly and turn it.

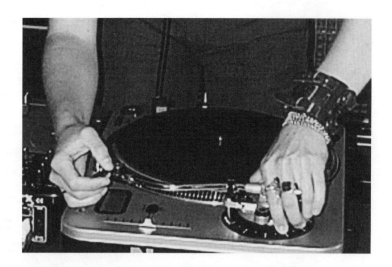

Fig. 2.6. Adjusting the tone-arm height

How you set up your tone arm depends on a few things, such as the cartridge and stylus you're using, your touch, and your individual style. DJ QBert likes to adjust the tone arm so the top of the cartridge is just above the surface of the record.

If any part of the stylus or cartridge other than the needle has contact with the record, your tone-arm height and weight adjustments aren't right, and things are going to skip.

Antiskating Control
Helps keep the needle from skipping, or skating, out of the record grooves by applying inward force to the tone arm. Most manuals advise setting the antiskating control to the same numeric setting as the tone-arm weight. If you increase the tone-arm weight by turning it around, try setting the antiskating control as high as it will go. Again, experiment to see what works best for you.

Dust Cover/Hinges
You'll want to remove the dust cover entirely before mixing. You can lift the dust cover out of its hinges by opening it first, then lifting it straight up. It's a good idea to put the dust cover on while transporting your turntable.

Belt Drive and Direct Drive Turntables

Turntables come in two basic varieties: belt drive and direct drive. Belt drive turntables use a belt, like the fan belt on a car, to turn the platter (the part that the record sits on). Separating the motor from the platter with a belt is an inexpensive way of reducing noise from the motor. This is why most inexpensive models are belt drive. However, there are high-quality belt drive turntables on the market, as well.

With direct drive turntables, a motor turns the platter directly. Because of this, the housing must be more robust and better at absorbing shock. This added heft also helps isolate the turntable from outside vibrations.

The better turntables of both varieties are generally heavier instruments.

What About That Old Turntable in the Basement?

There are plenty of stories about young DJs messing up their parents' old turntable while learning how to scratch. Turntables designed for use at home ("consumer" or "home" turntables) are missing many of the standard features of professional DJ turntables, such as a separate on/off switch and start/stop button, and variable pitch controls. DJ turntables also tend to have quicker start-up times than consumer turntables.

If you must start on a consumer turntable, remove the original rubber mat and replace it with a slip mat. The rubber mat is designed to provide friction to grip the record. The slip mat is designed to separate the record from the platter for scratching and cueing.

Always have an extra stylus on hand. If you're just starting out, it is likely that you may actually break the stylus on a consumer turntable. (I imagine that some of you reading this have already learned that the hard way.)

The instructions on scratching later in this book will help you avoid undue harm to your stylus. However, while all needles wear out eventually, scratching most certainly speeds up this process.

TIP

If you haven't yet looked ahead or seen a DJ scratch, be advised that "scratching" refers to manipulating the record while the needle is in the grooves, NOT pushing or dragging the needle across the grooves sideways! The latter will ruin both your records and your stylus in no time.

DJ Mixers

Inputs and Outputs

The typical DJ mixer has stereo inputs for two turntables and a microphone, and outputs for stereo headphones and for feeding either a home stereo, PA system, or recording console. Some mixers have extra stereo inputs for other sources, such as tape machines or CD players. More advanced mixers have additional outputs and inputs (known as "sends" and "returns") for hooking up external effects devices.

Fig. 2.7. Inputs and outputs for a basic DJ mixer

A turntable connection consists of two RCA connectors (left and right channels) and a ground wire connection. It's important to connect and hold the ground wire in place around the ground post by tightening the thumbscrew. If you don't connect the ground wire to the ground post, you'll get massive hum or buzz noises in your system.

Controls

The three controls used most often are the **crossfader**, for mixing the two turntables together, the **up-faders** or "volume faders," and the **on/off** switches on each turntable.

Fig. 2.8. Controls on a DJ mixer

TIP
You can't plug a turntable directly into a tape recorder or mixing board without going through a phono preamp first. The phono preamp boosts the output signal of the turntable cartridge. DJ mixers have these preamps built in, as do home stereo amplifier/receivers.

Additional controls include **gain controls**, to adjust the phono preamps for each turntable, **cue sends**, to route each turntable's signal to the headphones, and a **headphone volume control**, which does just what it says.

Many DJ mixers include **equalization** or **EQ** controls for each turntable. EQ controls let you shape the sound by adjusting the bass, midrange, and treble frequencies.

The most powerful EQ sections on DJ mixers can kill entire frequency ranges, giving you increased flexibility in creating arrangements. For instance, you could use a bass line while completely EQing out that record's high frequencies, which might include an undesirable cymbal sound.

Other bells and whistles on professional DJ mixers include built-in effects, automatic tempo sensing, and adjustable crossfader curves.

Playback Systems

You'll need to plug the outputs of your DJ mixer into an amplifier and speakers to hear what you're doing. On your DJ mixer, put the crossfader to the middle, set the channel switches to "phono" or "on," put the up-faders about halfway up. Keep the gain pots low at first, say a quarter of the way up.

VOLUME TIP
Experts tell us that what contributes most to hearing loss is exposure to high levels of volume for long periods of time. Keep your volume at reasonable levels. Carry earplugs with you when you go to concerts where you're not in charge of the volume level. I know many musicians who have suffered permanent hearing loss from their own constant playing of loud music, and not one of them thinks it was worth it.

Home Stereo
Plug into the "aux input" of your boom box or home stereo system's receiver/amplifier with two male-to-male RCA cables. Connect the other end to the output of your DJ mixer, which will be labeled "amplifier output" or something similar.

Make sure that the aux input is selected on your stereo system, and start with the volume all the way down. Play a record on one of your turntables, while slowly turning up the volume of your stereo system to a moderately low level. You should hear the record playing.

If you don't, check all of your controls and connections while keeping the volume on your stereo LOW! Chances are that you'll fix the problem by flipping a channel switch or something similar, and if you've jacked up the volume you could do serious damage to your speakers.

TAPE RECORDERS TIP
Many DJ mixers let you plug into a tape recorder at the same time. Most tape decks accept RCA or 1/4" inputs. Follow the instructions that came with your recording device to set your input levels.

PA System

The quality, size, and power of your PA system will be one of the determining factors in what kind of gigs you can handle.

Most professional DJ mixers provide low impedance (Low Z) outputs, often with 1/4" TRS (Tip Ring Sleeve) connections. You can plug these outputs directly into a professional amplifier's inputs, which are usually 1/4" jacks or three-pronged (XLR) connectors.

From the amplifier, the signal must be sent to speakers, usually through speaker cables with 1/4" ends or "banana plugs." If all of your cables have 1/4" ends, it's important to realize that there is a difference between speaker cables and the cables that go between your mixer and amplifier. It is a good idea to label all of your cables.

If you're playing at a large club, chances are there will be a house PA system. Many visiting DJs will bring in their own cartridges, and use the house turntables and mixer. If the club's setup is significantly different than your own, you may decide to use your own mixer and turntables. You should work this out with the club's management (and/or house DJ) before the gig.

If you are playing turntables in a band, you'll need to interface with the band's PA system. A few PA mixers have high impedance stereo inputs on RCA jacks, which are okay to use if you're very close (less than 10 feet) to the inputs. You're better off using 1/4" or XLR channel inputs. If your mixer only has RCA jacks, you may need to buy adapters or transformers.

Figure out what cables and adapters you'll need to connect to the PA you'll be working with well before the gig, and be sure to carry a few extra cables with you just in case.

Setting Up

In **standard mode** (fig. 2.9), the tone arms are accessible near the front of the turntable. This works fine for cueing and playing records.

Fig. 2.9. Standard mode

Most turntablists and scratch DJs set up their turntables with the tone arm across the top rather than on the side. This is commonly referred to as **battle mode** (Fig. 2.10).

Fig. 2.10. Battle mode

In battle mode, the tone arms are up and out of the way. This is more suited to scratching, beat juggling, and other techniques.

There are at least a dozen less common variations on these two setups, with names like the "duck rock mode" and the "left-handed lateral mode." While the majority of DJs starting out today gravitate towards standard or battle mode, you can execute the techniques in this book using any of the modes mentioned.

Slip Mats

Slip mats are 12-inch discs that go between the turntable's platter and the record. When you are scratching, cueing, or otherwise holding back the record while the turntable's platter is spinning, the slip mat serves as a buffer.

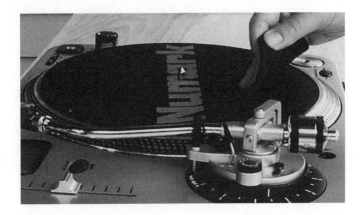

Fig. 2.11. Slip mat

Slip mats are often made of felt, often black (although they can be any color), and often have a logo or an advertisement emblazoned on them.

If your turntable came with a rubber mat to put on the platter (most do), don't use it. It will make scratching much more difficult. You most likely received one or two slip mats along with your DJ equipment. If not, they are inexpensive (a few bucks at the most) and available wherever DJ gear is sold.

Slip mats allow the turntable to spin while you manipulate the record. When you let go of the record, the slip mat and the record use gravity and friction to reconnect with the turntable's spinning platter and return to speed. You can help the record return to speed more quickly by giving a small, almost imperceptible nudge forward as you let go.

At first, it may seem hard to manipulate your records while the platter is spinning. The more you work with a particular record, the easier it will be to manipulate. This is known as "breaking in" a record.

The exercises later in the book will help you develop a smooth touch. In the meantime, there is another aid you can try.

Custom Plastic Slip Mats

An additional slip mat, made of clear plastic, is a tool that many turntablists find helpful. If you're having a hard time manipulating your records independently of the turntable's platter, try making your own plastic slip mat.

Fig. 2.12. Plastic slip mat

A plastic slip mat reduces the friction between the regular slip mat and the turntable's platter. The extra slippage a plastic slip mat provides may allow you to manipulate your records more easily.

All you'll need to make your own is a plastic sleeve from one of your record jackets, a pair of scissors (or a straight razor), a felt-tip pen (a Sharpie works fine), and a 12-inch record.

Find a thick plastic record sleeve (thicker is better). This can be the clear plastic sleeve that holds the record directly, or it can be the plastic sleeve that covers the record jacket, provided that it is thick enough to hold up to what we are about to do to it. You can also use wax paper.

1. First, cut the sleeve at the edges into two separate square pieces.

2. On a flat surface, place a 12-inch record directly on top of one of these squares. Center the record so that it doesn't hang over any of the edges.

Fig. 2.13. Outlining the record

3. Carefully outline the record on the plastic, using your felt-tip marker. Mark the center through the hole in the record. Using scissors, cut out the circle just inside the lines. Your custom plastic mat should be slightly smaller than your regular slip mat (12 inches).

Fig. 2.14. Trimming the shape

4. Use the sharp point of your pen to make a hole in the center of your plastic mat.

Fig. 2.15. Making the center hole

5. Place your newly-cut plastic slip mat onto the platter of your turntable.

Fig. 2.16. Custom plastic slip mat

6. Check the shape of the edges, and notice any imperfections in the circle that hang over the turntable's platter. Trim any parts that stick out, and make sure the hole in the center fits snugly over the turntable's stem.

7. Place the plastic slip mat on the platter, place a regular slip mat over it, then place a 12-inch record on top of both. Start the turntable spinning and apply enough pressure to the record to keep it from spinning while the platter keeps going.

You should notice an improvement in the ease of stopping and manipulating the record. In certain situations, the plastic slip mat may provide too much slippage. If you find this to be true, just take it off.

You can use the other half of your record sleeve to make a slip mat for your other turntable, if you plan to use both turntables for scratching.

It's also possible to cut out a plastic slip mat with a razor blade. If you choose to do this, be careful of whatever surface you are cutting on, as you're likely to cut it, too.

3. Preparing to Play

Which Hand Does What?

For most instruments, the formula is set. Take the guitar, for example. For right-handed players, the left hand is always on the guitar neck, while the right hand generates the sound by strumming, picking, or plucking the strings. Most lefties (like Jimi Hendrix and Paul McCartney) flip the guitar over and string it upside-down so their dominant hand still sets the strings in motion.

Unlike the guitar, a pair of turntables set up in battle mode is a symmetrical setup. Both hands have equal access to the records and the mixer.

When first starting to play turntables, many DJs use their dominant hand to manipulate the records, because that's where it seems all the action is. However, after playing for awhile, most realize how important the mixing hand is.

These days, scratch DJs do things with the crossfader that can be more intricate than what they do with the records. The fader hand plays sixteenth notes and triplets with lightning-fast techniques, such as the "crab" and the "transformer." Individual fingers strike the crossfader in a manner that resembles right-handed tremolo technique on the classical guitar.

Fig. 3.1. Intricate fader technique often attracts the DJ's dominant hand.

Once you start practicing these techniques, you may find it easier to use your nondominant hand to manipulate the record you're scratching and your dominant hand for the fast fader moves.

At first, right-handed beginning guitar students struggle with chords and fingerings in the left hand. It seems as though everything revolves around the neck of the guitar. It isn't long before the importance of the hand doing the picking takes over: quick strumming, intricate picking, tremolo. Many classical guitarists claim that playing the guitar is 90 percent right hand (the one that does the picking).

The same is true with the turntable/DJ mixer setup. At first, it may take all the coordination you have to get the records to behave the way you want. Eventually, though, the demands of the fader become more obvious.

Be Ambidextrous

It's important to develop the ability to manipulate the turntable and the DJ mixer with either hand. While your dominant hand may gravitate to the more difficult task, there are many situations where it pays to be a "switch hitter," as they say in baseball—able to use either hand. Beat juggling, sitting in with another DJ and sharing two turntables, and playing in a turntable ensemble are a few examples.

Fig. 3.2. Ambidextrous technique

For most of the exercises in this book, I refer to the "record hand" and the "mixer hand" (or "fader hand"), rather than the right hand and left hand.

Spend time practicing each technique with both hands. It will pay off.

Vital Vinyl

A companion record of beats and scratch material, *Turntable Technique* was made for this book. Side 2 contains all the scratching exercises taught in the book, so that you can hear and practice them by playing along.

With two copies of the *Turntable Technique* record, you can use the scratch material on one turntable to play along with the examples on the other turntable. Two copies will also allow you to beat match and mix the first two tracks on side 1, which have been specifically designed for this purpose. Owning two copies of the same record is a typical requirement for DJs, and it allows you to execute many beat juggling and mixing techniques.

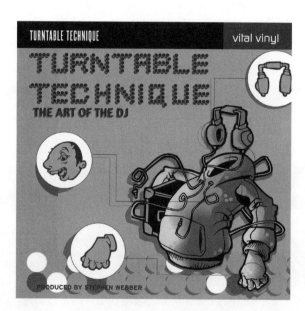

Fig. 3.3. *Turntable Technique* record jacket

For each exercise, I also describe the type of track to use, in case you don't have the *Turntable Technique* records.

As you progress, check out the whole series of *Vital Vinyl* records for fresh and original tools for the twenty-first-century DJ. You can purchase the records in the *Vital Vinyl* series on the Berklee Press Web site, www.berkleepress.com, or by calling Berklee Press directly, at (617) 747-2146.

4. Cueing Records

Cueing means finding the exact spot on a record to start playing. This could be the downbeat of track 1, the drum break of track 3, or the sound effect halfway into track 4 on side 2.

The tracks on a record are numbered from the outside moving in. The silent spaces between tracks show up as smooth areas that separate the tracks from each other.

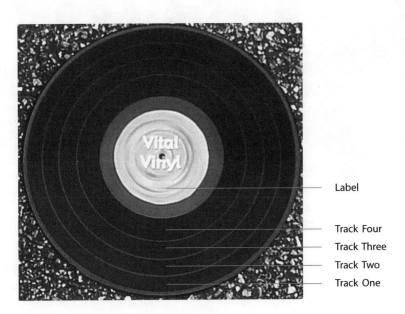

Fig 4.1. Record with tracks labeled

Using the Start/Stop Button

Back when vinyl records were played on the radio, DJs would cue them up and then set them in motion using the start/stop button. It's the easiest way to start getting the hang of it.

Side 1, track 1.

Let's start by cueing *Turntable Technique*, side 1, track 1. If you don't have this record, find one with a loud count-off or a strong downbeat at the top of side 1. Make sure your hands are clean (you don't want to get dirt all over your records!) and your playback system is on. On the mixer, turn the turntable's volume fader up and the crossfader to the center. Place the record on top of a slip mat on the turntable platter. Press the start/stop button on your turntable to start the platter spinning.

1. Carefully place the stylus at the beginning of the record.

2. As soon as you hear the first sound, press the start/stop button to stop the record from turning. You should hear the record quickly grind to a halt.

3. Ease your middle finger onto the record in the smooth space between the label and the end of the last track.

4. Rotate the record backwards (counterclockwise), until the stylus is at the beginning of the track. This is called **backspinning**. You should hear what's on the record (in this case, the count-off) going backwards.

Figs. 4.2a–c. Backspinning

5. Rotate the record forward (clockwise) until you hear the first sound on the record (in this case, the word "one").

6. Rock the record back and forth until you locate the exact beginning of the track.

7. Back the record up slightly to give the turntable space to get up to speed. You're now ready to play the track.

8. Press the start/stop button to play the track.

Listen carefully to make sure that the record is up to speed by the time the audio begins. If you hear the pitch sliding into the first "one," back up more in step 7. If there is too much time before the record starts, back up less in step 7.

Repeat these steps until you get the hang of it. With practice you'll get to know exactly how much space your turntable needs to get up to speed.

On the Fly

You can also set the starting place for a record by hand, while the platter is spinning. This allows you to cue things up quickly, on the fly. With the platter already spinning, the record can get back up to speed faster. Here's how:

1. Place the stylus at the beginning of the already-spinning record.

2. As soon as you hear the first sound on the record, gently rest your middle finger on the smooth area between the label and the last track.

3. Apply just enough pressure to drag the record to a stop while the platter continues to turn underneath.

4. Backspin the record to the start of the track.

5. Rotate the record forward again (clockwise) until you hear the first sound on the record. You may want to rock the record back and forth until you locate the exact beginning of the track, applying slight pressure to the body of the record.

6. Set the record in motion in such a way that it instantly returns to playing speed. Rather than lifting your hand straight up, release the record by moving your finger tips slightly in a forward direction.

Fig. 4.3a. Grasping the body of the record   **Fig. 4.3b.** Releasing the record

If you hear the record sliding up to speed, work on your release. Make sure you're not pushing down too hard and slowing the platter. If the record seems too fast for the first moment of playback (if the voice saying "one" sounds like it's on helium), back off on your forward nudge.

Practice cueing by hand until the technique becomes second nature. This could take dozens of spins, so be patient!

Cueing in Time

Side 1, track 1.

"In time" means that you are right in sync with the tempo of whatever you're playing along with. As you move on to mixing, blending, and beat matching, it's important that you can start a record in time. The following procedure can help you develop this skill:

1. Play the first few bars of track 1 of *Turntable Technique* (or enough of the track you're working with to get a feel for the tempo).

2. Keep tapping your foot or nod your head in time with the beat as you backspin and cue the record.

3. Now, while holding the record, count down in time with the track, "One! Two! Three! Four!" rocking the record back and forth slightly with each beat.

4. Set the record in motion an instant before the next beat, so that the record starts perfectly in time with your countdown.

Repeat these steps until you can nail it every time.

Fig. 4.4. Setting the record in motion

Marking Records

Marking records helps you visualize the beginning of a track. This is incredibly helpful when beat matching, beat juggling, or even just cueing records. Often, having a record marked can reduce or even negate the need for headphones.

Most DJs mark their record with an adhesive label or tape. Cassette labels and adhesive dots are two favorites. You can buy adhesive dots at office and educational supply stores. Never use tape that has gummy adhesive (like masking tape, duct tape, or packing tape).

To mark the beginning of track 1, first locate the exact beginning of the track. (Follow the steps in "Cueing Using the Start/Stop Button.") When you locate the exact beginning of the track, put your marker on the outer edge of the label.

Fig. 4.5. Marking a record using an adhesive dot at the stylus

There is no real standard place to mark a record. Some DJs will put the dot or cassette label at 12 o'clock, others will have it point to the stylus illumination light, the stylus itself, or even the on/off switch.

My advice is to experiment. Place your mark somewhere, try cueing the record a few times, then move the mark somewhere else and try cueing some more. Leave your mark wherever it works best for your particular hand-eye coordination.

You can also mark the location of a specific word, sound effect, or other audio event by placing a piece of tape on the track itself, right next to the targeted sound. Use a smaller piece of tape, and make sure the corners are pressed down securely so the tape won't come into contact with the head shell as it passes over. Start by placing the tape exactly one groove out from the targeted sound, but experiment to see what works best in each situation.

Fig. 4.6. Marking the exact location of a sound

White artist's tape work especially well, and leaves no residue. This allows you to move the tape around until you find the exact spot.

5.

Beat Matching

Beat matching means getting two records perfectly in sync with each other. You can then use the crossfader to switch between them. Beat matching is a skill that every DJ must master. When you're playing a rave, party, dance, or club, being able to segue (move smoothly) from one tune to another without losing the beat will help you keep the dance floor full. Beat matching must be second nature if you are going to get into beat juggling, a main component of many scratch-mixing routines.

You can beat match any two records that are close to the same tempo and have complementary beats by adjusting the variable pitch controls on each turntable. It's a good idea to write down the tempos of the different tracks in your collection on the record label or sleeve, or on a list you keep with your records.

Tempos are expressed in beats per minute (bpm). There are devices that can help you find the bpm of any song. For instance, the "Dr. Beat" metronome by Boss lets you tap along with the beat to find the tempo. "Dr. Beat" displays the bpm numerically after four taps. There are other devices that detect bpm automatically, like the "Beatkeeper" by Numark. A few DJ mixers even have them built in.

The easiest way to start getting the hang of beat matching is to get two identical copies of the same record playing in time with each other. Since the tempos on both records are exactly the same, you can practice cueing before you start having to also use the variable pitch controls to precisely match beats.

Begin by cueing up two copies of the *Turntable Technique* record (or two copies of another record) to the very beginning of side 1, track 1. (Follow the steps in the section, "Cueing Using the Start/Stop Buttons.") When the records are cued up:

1. Start the record on your right and let it play.

2. Get yourself in sync with the beat. (Tap your foot, nod your head, etc.)

3. With the index, middle, and ring fingers of your left hand, press down on the record. Use your thumb to press the start/stop button.

Side 1, track 1.

4. Let the platter spin up to speed while you keep the record from moving.

5. Count down four beats, then spin the record you're holding at just the right moment to synchronize the beats on the two records.

Fig. 5.1. Starting the platter while holding the record

If you miss, you can just let the record on your right keep playing, backspin the record on your left to the top, and try setting it in motion again. You may have to try this several times before you get the two records in perfect sync.

Let's say you've gotten both records going and you're close to being perfectly in sync, but not quite. Rather than stopping one of the records, you can use one of the following techniques.

Spinning the Label

1. Decide which record is behind. (The headphones can be helpful for this.)

2. Place your middle finger on the label of the record that's behind, spinning your finger along with the record.

3. Let your finger spin a little faster, pushing the record along with it.

4. Listen closely to determine when you have gotten the two records in sync—or if you're getting farther apart!

Fig. 5.2. a, b, and c. Spinning the label

Dragging the Platter

1. Determine which record is ahead.

2. Drag your middle finger against the side of the platter that the record is on, slowing down the record slightly.

3. Listen closely to determine when the two records are in sync—or whether they're getting farther apart!

Fig. 5.3. Dragging the platter

Get on in there and spin and drag up a storm until you've gotten the hang of it. Once you get comfortable with these techniques, beat matching becomes a breeze.

You may need to use the variable pitch control on your turntables to perfectly match beats on two records. If you are matching beats on two different songs, you will almost always need the variable pitch control. Some DJs get two records in sync using only the variable pitch control, speeding up and slowing down the record without spinning the label or dragging the platter.

Tips:

- Use a metronome, drum machine, or beat-sensing device to determine the bpm of the songs or beats you want to work with, and write the tempos down. Once you choose two songs to beat match, write down the variable pitch settings you're using to put them in sync.

- There are dots on the side of the platter that are lit by a colored light (often red or pink) on most DJ turntables. When the turntable is operating at exactly 33-1/3 or 45 rpm, the dots look like they are standing still.

- As you scratch, hold, spin, drag, or adjust the pitch of your records, watch the dots to see when the record speed changes. If the dots look like they are staying still, the record's speed is not changing. The faster the dots seem to move, the more you are slowing down or speeding up the record.

- When two copies of the same record are close to being in sync, the records will sound "phased." Or, if the records are already in sync, when they start to sound phased, it's a sign that they are drifting apart. You can also use this sound, also referred to as "flanging," as a musical effect.

Cueing with Headphones

When you're mixing for an audience, you'll probably want to be able to cue a record without the audience hearing it. This is where headphone cueing comes in.

Suppose you want to get the next record ready to play on the left turntable while your audience is hearing the record playing on the right turntable.

1. Make sure the crossfader is all the way over to the right.

2. Set the mixer's cue switch to monitor the left turntable (often labeled Ch-1 or Program-1) in your headphones.

3. Listening through your headphones, cue up the record on the left turntable. (Follow the steps in the previous sections.)

Make sure the volume fader is up for the left turntable (Ch-1 or Program-1).

When you're ready for the audience to hear the next record, use the cross-fader to "segue" (pronounced seg-way, meaning, to transition smoothly) between the two records.

Practice cueing with headphones for both the right and left turntables.

TIPS

If you are matching the beat of the record in your head-phones to a record that's playing over the sound sys-tem, slide one ear out of the headphones as you cue it up, so you can hear both records. There are headphones made just for DJs that have only one earpiece.

Fig. 5.4. Cueing with headphones, one ear off

Creative Mixing

How you put together and mix a set is a big part of what defines your style.

Edan, a talented Boston DJ and MC, suggests, "Look for tracks that comple-ment each other, and mix them in a way that pays tribute to the music."

Records containing "club mixes" often feature long, unstructured intros and out-ros that allow DJs to crossfade in and out of records without matching beats.

When you do beat match two different songs, you can do some creative mix-ing by using the crossfader to go back and forth between the two.

Side 1, track 1.
Side 1, track 2.

To start getting the hang of this, beat match *Turntable Technique*, side 1, track 1 with side 1, track 2 of a second copy of the record. While there are differ-ent elements in each track, both tracks share the same tempo.

Mix the tracks together for awhile, then crossfade back and forth between the two, making sure that the sync between the two remains solid. Try slamming the crossfader back and forth every eight bars, every four bars, every two bars, every bar, every two beats, every beat, and every half beat! Be creative and create your own arrangement. (See Chapter 7 for help on musical terminology.)

You can also use more advanced crossfader techniques such as the "crab" and the "transformer" (described later in this book) when mixing beats.

Search your record collection for other songs and tracks to play together. Remember, the variable pitch control on your turntables can help match tempos between songs where the tempos aren't the same.

Build up your record collection, and develop your own style, your own taste. Most of all, enjoy yourself!

b. The Basic Scratch

The **basic scratch** is also known as the "baby scratch." For the basic scratch, you only manipulate the record, not the fader. You can scratch virtually any sound, with a wide variety of results.

Side 1, track 4.

We'll start out using *Turntable Technique*, side 1, track 4. It's useful to have a track like this, with plenty of sustained sound, in case the needle skips to a different part of the track. If you don't have *Turntable Technique*, use a record that has a track with constant white noise.

On the mixer, put the volume fader up and the crossfader to the center.

Playing the Basic Scratch

1. Place the record on top of a slip mat on the turntable's platter.

2. Press the start/stop button to start the platter spinning.

3. Carefully place the stylus at the beginning of the track.

4. Let the white noise play for a few seconds.

5. Press the start/stop button again to stop the record.

6. Place the tips of your index, middle, and ring fingers on the record, and slowly drag the record back and forth. Keep your wrist relaxed and your motions fluid.

Congratulations, you're scratching! Experiment with scratching at different speeds. Improvise (make up) different rhythms.

Study the following pictures, as well as figures 7.7 and 7.8 in the next chapter, for correct hand position.

Fig. 6.1. Basic scratch (forward)   **Fig. 6.2.** Basic scratch (back)

The pitch of the scratch (how high or low it is) depends on two things: the pitch of the recorded track, and the speed that you are dragging the record. Notice the changing pitch of the sound as you alter the speed of your scratch.

The volume of the scratch also depends on two things: how high you set the faders on the mixer, and how fast you drag the record (the velocity of the scratch).

On lightweight, less expensive turntables, the tone arms may tend to bounce, skipping the needle to different sections of the track, or sometimes even to different tracks. Skipping can be a signal that you are pushing down too hard, bouncing the record.

To avoid skipping, lighten your touch. Turn the record with your fingers, moving it smoothly back and forth with only a slight, constant pressure. Let your fingers pivot. Remember, no bouncing!

Tips:

- Practice on both turntables.

- Practice both hands.

- While improvising rhythms, remember that the silence between the notes is just as important as the notes themselves.

- Use a light touch to reduce skipping.

Adding a Beat

Side 1, track 2.

When you feel comfortable with the basic scratch, try adding a beat on the second turntable and playing along.

On the mixer, raise the volume faders for both turntables, and set the cross-fader to the center. On your second turntable, cue up a second copy of *Turntable Technique* to side 1, track 2. This track features a groove that is perfect to scratch over. You can also experiment with other tracks that have medium-tempo grooves and some musical space you can fill with scratch rhythms.

Be tasteful, and try phrasing your scratches like a melody or a conversation.

7. Reading Rhythms

If you already read music, the following pages will be a review. If you've never read music before, now is the time to start! As you develop your scratching techniques, why not simultaneously learn the vocabulary of the universal language called music?

Sure, you can play the turntables without reading music, just like you can speak without being able to read English. But reading music will help you to communicate with other musicians. In this case, it will help me to communicate to you specific information about playing the turntables.

This book makes reading music easy. You may be surprised to find out how much you already know!

Beats and Bars

Music is sound that happens in time. In most cases, we divide that time into small segments, called **beats**. Beats are grouped together into **bars** (or "measures"). In most hip-hop and rock, there are usually four beats in a bar.

Think of a bar as a dollar. Each beat is a quarter. In fact, the kind of note that gets one beat (most of the time) is called a **quarter note**.

The quarter note looks like this:

Fig. 7.1. Quarter note

When you write words on notebook paper, you write from left to right on a single line. Music is also written from left to right, on something called a **staff**. The staff is divided into bars by vertical lines called (you guessed it)

bar lines. The standard staff has five lines, which are used to indicate pitches. For the exercises in this book, we'll use a single-line staff.

Fig. 7.2. Standard staff with five lines

Fig. 7.3. Scratch staff

The time signature comes at the beginning of every piece of music. The top number tells you how many beats there will be in each bar, while the bottom number tells you what kind of note gets one beat.

Fig. 7.4. Time signature

For example, in 4/4 time, there are four beats in each bar (or measure), and the quarter note receives one full beat. The vast majority of r&b, rock, and hip-hop tunes are in 4/4 time.

There are lots of other time signatures. If you remember that the top number tells you the number of beats in a bar, and the bottom number tells you which note receives one full beat, then you can read any time signature. For example, in 2/4 time, there are two beats in each bar (or measure) and the quarter note gets one beat.

The clef is a symbol at the beginning of a piece of music that tells you about the lines and spaces. The neutral clef (sometimes called the "percussion clef") shows that staff positions do not represent precise pitches.

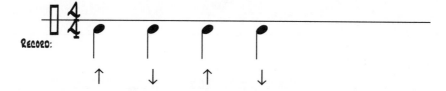

Fig. 7.5. The neutral clef

Forward and Backward Strokes

The notes that represent the movements of the record are written below the staff. The arrows that show the direction of the turntable hand are written below these notes.

Fig. 7.6. Forward and backward strokes

An arrow pointing up indicates a forward stroke, pushing the record away from you.

Fig 7.7. Forward stroke

An arrow pointing down indicates a backward stroke, pulling the record towards you.

Fig. 7.8. Backward stroke

Rests

There are also symbols called **rests**, which tell you when not to play. The kind of rest that tells you not to play for one beat (in 4/4 time) is called the **quarter rest**. (See a pattern emerging here?)

𝄽

Fig. 7.9. Quarter rest

The **repeat signs** tells you to go back and play it again.

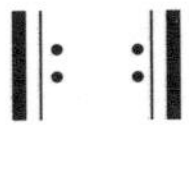

𝄆 ⦂ 𝄇

Fig. 7.10. Repeat sign

8. Scratching Exercises

This section contains exercises to practice your scratching techniques. The *Turntable Technique* records contain all the exercises in order, starting on side 2, track 1.

To play along with exercises 1 through 6, play *Turntable Technique*, side 2, track 1 on one turntable. On the second turntable, use side 1, track 4 of your second copy of *Turntable Technique* to scratch. You can also use white noise from another record on the second turntable.

Quarter Note Exercises

For exercises 1 through 6, play along with side 2, track 1.

Play the following exercises using quarter notes and rests, alternating forward and backward strokes. It's important that you keep silent during rests. Don't just slow down your scratch, stop it altogether.

■ **Exercise 1**

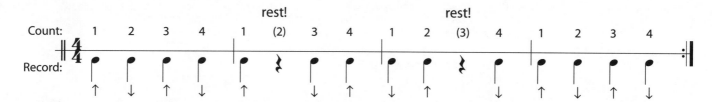

■ **Exercise 2**

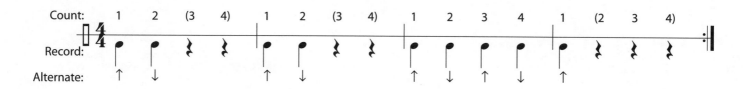

48

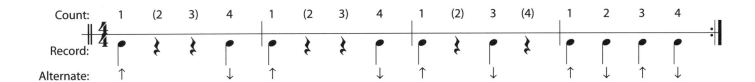

Expand Your Palette of Sounds

Once you get the hang of scratching with the constant white noise on track 4, try scratching with something more challenging. Cue up side 1, track 3. Let the first spoken words go by. When you get to the blast of noise, stop the record by pressing the start/stop button, and backspin to cue it up.

Try scratching using only this short blast of noise. This will force you to become more accurate with your scratching, and be aware of when your needle is skipping.

Get comfortable with where the noise starts and ends. You can set up visual cues by marking the beginning and end of the sound on your record with part of a cassette label or adhesive dots.

Start by doing short strokes that stay in the middle of the noise. Then try doing longer strokes that play all of the way through the noise, where you can hear the noise's definite beginning and ending.

Eventually, you'll be able to work with any sound, no matter how long or short. You may want to scratch a kick or snare drum sound, a bass note, or an individual spoken word. Anything you can find on a record, you can scratch!

Eighth Note Exercises

An eighth note looks like this:

Fig. 8.1. Eighth note

In 4/4 time, the eighth note receives half a beat.

Two eighth notes together look like this:

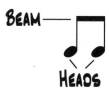

Fig. 8.2. Two eighth notes

You must play two eighth notes (forward and back) within the time it took you to play a single quarter note—one full beat.

Count the beats out loud. Call every other eighth note "and," as in "one-and-two-and-three-and-four-and." For example:

Fig. 8.3. Counting eighth notes

Generally, the numbered beats are the downbeats, the "ands" represent the upbeats.

For exercises 4 through 6, play along with side 2, track 1.

Play the following exercises, which combine quarter and eighth notes. Alternate forward and backward strokes.

■ **Exercise 4**

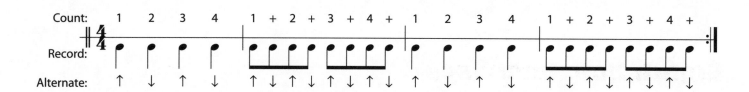

■ **Exercise 5**

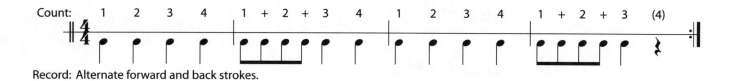

Record: Alternate forward and back strokes.

■ **Exercise 6**

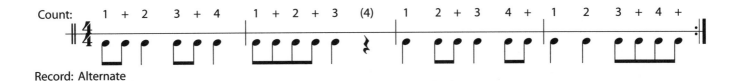

Syncopation

Scratching by QBert, MixMaster Mike, DJ Swamp, and practically all good DJs is full of **syncopation**. This is where it starts getting interesting!

Syncopation refers to rhythms where the attack, normally falling on a down-beat, is moved earlier. The effect of this **anticipation** is to give the rhythm a bit of a **push**.

To accomplish this, we'll need to learn one new symbol, the **eighth rest**:

𝄾

Fig. 8.4. Eighth rest

Like the eighth note, the eighth rest lasts for half a beat. The difference, of course, is that the eighth rest represents silence.

Syncopation Exercises

The syncopation exercises combine quarter notes, eighth notes, quarter rests, and eighth rests. Be sure to count your "and's" ("one-and-two-and-three-and-four-and"), so you can nail the syncopation.

For exercises 7 to 9, use side 2, track 2.

■ **Exercise 7**

The first beat of the second and fourth measures are anticipated by the eighth notes on the "and" of 4 from the previous measures.

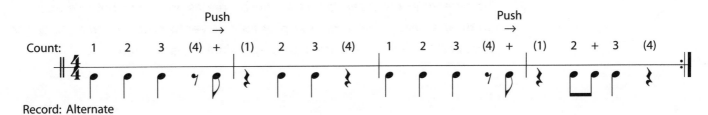

■ **Exercise 8**

In exercise 8, the third beat of each measure is anticipated by eighth notes landing on the "and" of 2.

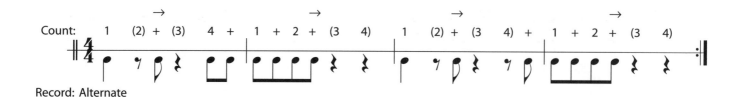

Record: Alternate

The eighth notes landing on the "and" of 4 in the first and third bars are not anticipations, because new notes are executed on the downbeats of the following measures.

■ **Exercise 9**

Except for the first note, everything you play in exercise 9 is an anticipation.

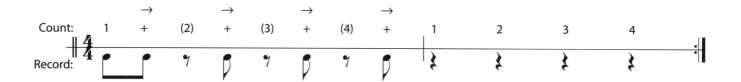

Don't be frustrated if these syncopated rhythms don't come to you right away. Move on to the next chapter; the rhythms there are actually easier! Come back and review, playing along with the exercises on the record. Eventually, syncopation will become second nature to you.

Sixteenth Note Exercises

The **sixteenth note** looks like this:

Fig. 8.5. Sixteenth note

The sixteenth note receives half as much time as an eighth note, or one fourth of a beat in 4/4 time. You play four sixteenth notes (forward, back, forward, back) in the time it takes to play a single quarter note.

To count sixteenth notes, add a long "e" sound after each beat, and add an "ah" sound after the "and." For example, "one-e-and-a, two-e-and-a."

To play along with exercises 10 to 13, cue up side 2, track 2.

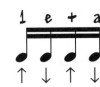

Fig. 8.6. Counting four sixteenth notes

■ **Exercise 10**

This exercise starts with quarter notes, moves on to eighth notes, then sixteenth notes, then works its way back to quarters.

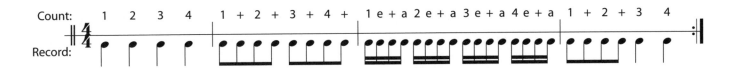

Exercises 11 and 12 mix quarter notes, eighth notes, and sixteenth notes.

■ **Exercise 11**

■ **Exercise 12**

■ **Exercise 13**

This exercise adds in quarter rests and eighth rests.

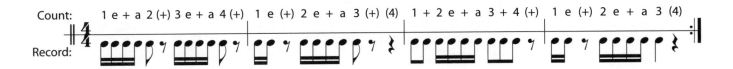

Silence and Dynamics

In his commencement speech here at the Berklee College of Music, composer and recording artist Sting advised the graduates that it is the "space between the notes" that is most important. A constant barrage of notes without the contrast of silence will become boring and tedious in no time.

So, let's learn more about rests:

Whole, Half, and Sixteenth Note Rests

A whole note rest lasts four beats. In 4/4 time, this is a whole bar, which makes it easy to remember. A whole note rest looks like this:

Fig. 8.7. Whole note rest

To remember what a whole rest looks like, think of it as so heavy (being four whole beats long) that it sinks below the line.

A half note rest lasts two beats. In 4/4 time, this is half of a bar. It looks like this:

Fig. 8.8. Half note rest

To remember what the half rest looks like, remember that it's not quite as heavy as the whole rest, so it sits on top of the line.

Sixteenth note rests last one-fourth of a beat, just like a sixteenth note.

It looks like this:

Fig. 8.9. Sixteenth note rest

Dynamics refers to the volume of a musical passage. Mastering dynamics is key to expressing yourself musically. It is no surprise that DMC world champion DJ Craze is considered a master in his use of dynamics.

A **crescendo** indicates that the music should get louder, increasing the volume. A **decrescendo** indicates that the music should get quieter, decreasing the volume.

Fig. 8.10. Crescendo and decrescendo

Obviously, manipulating the up-fader will change your volume. This is an effective way to execute a crescendo or decrescendo.

You can also increase the volume of a scratch by using more velocity. The more area of a record you cover in a set amount of time, the louder the scratch; the less record you use, the lower the volume.

Try scratching sixteenth notes back and forth, increasing and decreasing the velocity of your scratch to create a crescendo and decrescendo.

Fig 8.11. Sixteenth notes with dynamics

Playing Fills

DJs who play with bands (like DJ Swamp who plays with Beck, and DJ Lethal of Limp Bizkit), will often play fills on the turntable between vocal phrases. These could be simple or complex, and could use any number of sounds, including words from the song.

■ **Exercise 14: Fills**

This exercise will give you some examples of simple fills to use between musical phrases. Here you're laying out—not playing—every other bar, then filling for a bar. Be sure to get louder during the crescendo and softer during the decrescendo.

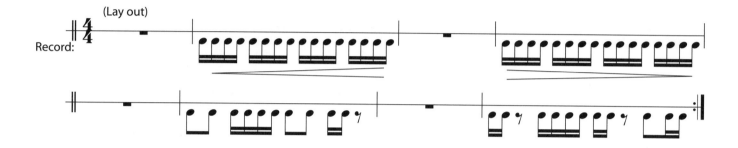

You can practice fills by playing along with almost any record. On *Turntable Technique*, the first two tracks on side 1 are perfect for filling in between musical phrases. Use a variety of sounds and rhythms.

Moving On

Don't expect everything to fall into place at once. Mastering the turntable, like any instrument, takes time and practice. Repetition is key. You'll make more progress if you play often (every day, if possible), rather than practicing only once a week for a long time.

Play through new exercises slowly at first, counting out loud. You can play along slowly with the examples by turning the variable pitch control all the way down on your second turntable.

9. Mixer Exercises

Playing the Up-Fader

The **up-fader** (or "volume fader") adds another dimension to playing the turntable. DJ mixers come with two or more up-faders, to control the volume of each turntable. They can be labeled CH-1 and CH-2 for channels 1 and 2, and PGM 1 and PGM 2 for programs 1 and 2, or something similar.

Up-fader, Channel 1

Up-fader, Channel 2

Fig. 9.1. Up-faders

Side 1, track 5.

First, let's get the hang of using the up-fader musically, in rhythm:

1. Cue up side 1 track 5 of *Turntable Technique*, which has a continuous tone.

2. Adjust the mixer's gain controls and your playback system so the tone is at a decent level when the volume fader is set all the way up. It should be loud enough to function as a bass instrument, but not deafening.

3. Put the crossfader into the center.

4. Turn the channel's switch to the "on" or "phono" position.

5. Starting with the up-fader all the way down, use your thumb to push it up to the top in one quick, smooth motion.

6. Use your index finger to push the up-fader back down to zero in another quick, smooth motion.

You should hear the fader click as it hits the top and the bottom of its range.

Repeat steps 5 and 6 with both hands, keeping your wrist loose.

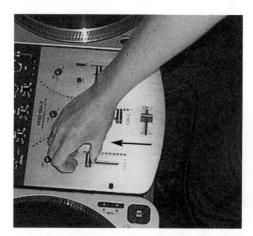 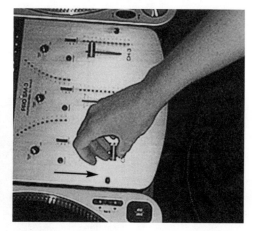

Fig. 9.2a. Up-fader up   **Fig. 9.2b.** Up-fader down

See how fast you can thrust the up-fader up and down. Try leaving it up for different lengths of time, playing longer notes and shorter notes. Remember to keep your fingers, wrist, and arm relaxed.

Cue up and play a beat on your second turntable. Improvise some rhythms with the volume fader on the first turntable over the beats from the second turntable.

Try using other tones. The last cut on each side of all volumes of the *Vital Vinyl* records have continuous tones or sounds. You can also use white noise, like a train or babbling brook from *Turntablist's Toolkit*. The *Vital Vinyl* record *Beat Bomb* is an excellent source of beats to play tones over.

Reading Fader Moves

Fader moves are written on the top of the staff. The length of each note is determined by how long the fader is up, so each note represents two moves: the fader being turned up (the attack of the note), and the fader being turned down (the release of the note).

The following exercises are for the fader only. We'll combine the two hands in the next chapter. As always, practice the exercises with both hands.

Play along with exercises 15 to 17 on *Turntable Technique,* **side 2, track 4.**

■ **Exercise 15**

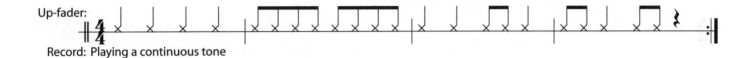

Up-fader:

Record: Playing a continuous tone

Triplets

Triplets slice a beat into three equal parts, rather than two. Three eighth note triplets must be played in one beat, the same space of time given to two regular eighth notes.

Fig. 9.3. Eighth note triplets

Exercises 16 and 17 use eighth note triplets.

■ **Exercise 16**

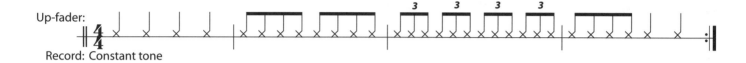

■ **Exercise 17**

Playing the Switch

Located at the top of the up-fader is the **channel switch**, also known as the "on/off switch," the "phono-line switch," or simply, the "switch." To play the switch, make sure the up-fader is up and the crossfader is near the center.

Fig. 9.4. Playing the switch

Side 1, track 5.

Play a constant tone, such as the one on side 1, track 5 of *Turntable Technique*. Practice turning the switch on and off to play notes of different lengths, just like you did with the up-fader. Have some fun improvising. Remember to keep your fingers, wrist, and arm relaxed. Try moving between the switch and the up-fader.

Play along with exercises 18 and 19 on side 2, track 4.

Rhythms written for the switch are written on top of the staff like those written for the up-fader. During a rest, the switch is off. If the eighth note triplets seem too fast at first, slow down the record on your second turntable to a comfortable speed. Be sure to work both hands.

■ **Exercise 18**

■ **Exercise 19**

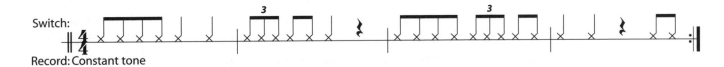

Additional Practice

Once you master these exercises, go back to exercises 1–14 and practice playing the scratch rhythms using the switch and the up-fader.

10. Articulation

Articulation refers to exactly *how* a note is executed, for example, whether the note is played short, long, or accented.

Staccato notes are played very short. While the amount of time the note receives will stay the same, only the first portion of that time will be occupied with sound. The remainder of the note's time will be given to silence.

The actual sound of a quarter note played staccato is more like a sixteenth note followed by enough rests to take up the remainder of the beat. The staccato articulation is represented by a dot placed above the note. It's easier to read and count longer notes marked staccato than it would be to write in all the rests necessary to obtain the same sound.

Fig. 10.1. Staccato

Playing **legato** is the opposite of staccato. Legato notes take up the whole time allotted to them, and are as connected as possible to the next note.

A line above the note represents the tenuto articulation. This line means to play especially legato: full value, long, full, broad notes.

Fig. 10.2. Tenuto

Accented notes are played louder and with more emphasis than normal. The **short accent** (sometimes called a "housetop") tells you to play the note short and hard, like a loud staccato. The **long accent** tells you to play the note long and hard, for the full beat.

Play along with exercises 20 and 21 on side 2, track 4.

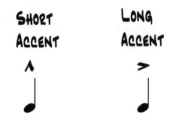

Fig. 10.3. Short and long accents

■ **Exercise 20**

Try this articulation exercise using the basic scratch:

What is the difference between a staccato and a short accent when using the up-fader, if they both involve hitting the top of the fader path every time? Nothing.

In exercise 21, when you play unaccented notes, don't push the fader up all the way. When you play accented notes, go ahead and push the fader up all the way, until you hear it click. The accented notes will sound louder.

With practice, you'll get comfortable using the whole range of dynamics available to you with the up-fader.

■ **Exercise 21**

Try the following articulation exercise using the up-fader.

11. Combining Both Hands

So far, we've been working with the record and the fader separately, and with good reason. The old adage "divide and conquer" isn't just about strategy on the battlefield. Breaking a new skill down into individual parts is just as helpful in learning to play the turntable as it is in learning the martial arts, or playing the piano.

The next several techniques will use both hands, combining fader moves and record manipulations. If you are having trouble with any of these techniques at first, try practicing each hand separately.

Also, be sure to review the exercises we've gone through so far. Use different sounds in your scratching, and find progressively faster break beats to work out over.

The Stab

The **stab** is a short and powerful burst of sound, executed by coordinating abrupt motions of both the fader and the record. Both hands must work together. To execute the stab:

Side 1, track 4 or 5.

1. Cue up continuous sound, like the white noise of *Turntable Technique*, side 1, track 4, or the tone of *Turntable Technique*, side 1, track 5.

2. Start with the up-fader down all the way.

3. Hold the record still, letting the platter spin underneath.

4. Push the record away from you (executing a forward stroke) while simultaneously throwing the fader up.

5. Immediately pull the fader back down

6. Pull the record back towards you (executing a back stroke) in silence.

Figs. 11.1a. and 11.1b. The stab

Steps 4 through 6 happen in one quick, violent motion, thus the name: "the stab." Note that both hands are moving in the same direction at the same time, making this one of the easier scratching techniques to coordinate.

The stab is most effective when you only hear the forward stroke. Make sure that you bring the fader down quickly to mute the sound of the back stroke.

If you have trouble keeping the platter spinning while you hold the record, you can also execute the stab with the platter at rest. However, you should work on getting the hang of letting the platter spin while you manipulate the record. You will soon be combining the stab with other techniques that require a spinning platter.

Sometimes it's easier to get a grip closer to the label. Do this when you need to, but work on getting comfortable grabbing the record anywhere without slowing the platter. If the illuminated dots on the side of the platter appear stationary, then the platter is spinning up to speed.

For exercises 22 through 26, play along with side 2, track 5.

Before attempting the following exercises, work on making your stabs concise. Listen to the stabs on the record to be sure yours are sounding tight. Remember, you want to mute the entire back stroke by quickly bringing down the fader.

■ **Exercise 22**

Stabs are short and accented. Practice the following exercises using the stab.

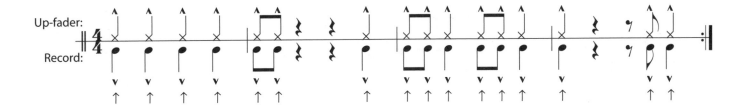

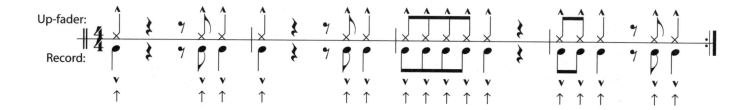

Quarter Note Triplets

Three quarter note triplets take up the same amount of time as two regular quarter notes. With quarter note triplets, you'll be splitting two beats (half of a bar) into three equal parts.

Fig. 11.2. Quarter note triplet

Practice the following exercises using the stab.

Play along with side 2, track 5.

Stabs with triplets

■ **Exercise 24**

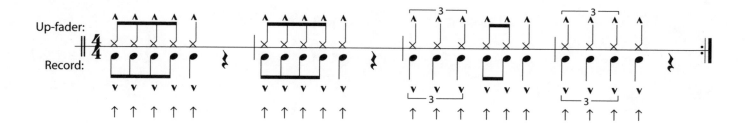

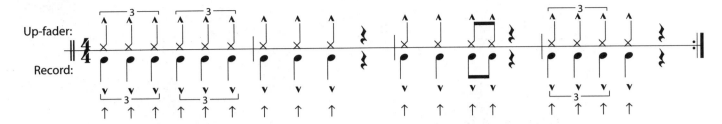

Stabs with the Switch

You can perform stabs (and other scratching techniques) using the switch instead of the fader. The switch gives you a sharper, more precise sound, because the signal comes on instantly at full power, rather than fading in and out. Play exercises 24 and 25 again, this time using the switch instead of the fader.

The Back Stab

The **back stab** is just like the stab, except the sound is played backwards. The record hand performs a back stroke while the fader or the switch is on. With the back stab, you mute the forward scrape by pulling down the fader or turning off the switch. Your hands move in opposite directions.

If you're using a continuous tone or noise, cue into the center. If you're using a shorter sound, make sure you're already into that sound so it will play (backwards) as you execute a backward stroke.

1. Cue up the sound you intend to use.

2. Start with the up-fader down all the way.

3. Hold the record still, letting the platter spin underneath.

4. Pull the record towards you (executing a backward stroke), while simultaneously throwing the fader up.

5. Immediately pull the fader back down.

6. Push the record away from you (executing a forward stroke) in silence.

Figs. 11.3a. and 11.3b. The back stab

Instead of both hands moving the same way, your hands are moving in opposite directions. We'll start with an easy exercise to let you get the hang of it. Try it first with the up-fader. After you get the hang of it, move to the switch. Remember, we want to hear all back strokes.

Play along with side 2, track 5.

■ **Exercise 26**

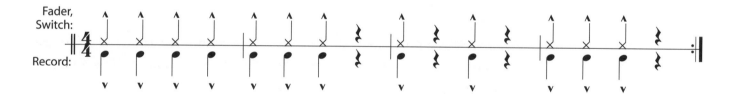

Scratching with Continuous Eighth Notes

A great way to ease into more complex scratches is to keep your record hand moving in continuous eighth notes while your fader hand creates rhythms. This is also known as the "military scratch."

Start by using continuous noise, like the white noise of *Turntable Technique*, side 1, track 4, or the tone on side 1, track 5. If you're feeling more adventurous (and you have decent control in your record hand), pick out a sound effect or spoken word from side 1, track 3.

1. Cue up the sound you intend to use.

2. Start with the up-fader down all the way.

3. Move the record in constant eighth notes, alternating forward and back strokes, letting the platter spin underneath.

Fig. 11.4. Continuous eighth notes

4. Play a variety of rhythms with the up-fader, leaving it up for one to several strokes.

The key is to keep the turntable moving in constant eighth notes: "forward, back, forward, back, forward, back, forward, back"; "one-and-two-and-three-and-four-and."

Play eighth notes with the fader up, slowly at first. Then try pulling the fader down for every other group of four eighth notes. Be precise with your fader moves. Cut off immediately after four eighth notes. Don't let an extra half scratch go by before you move the fader down to zero.

Once you master this, let groups of two eighth notes play with the fader up, then two with the fader down. Then try improvising your own rhythms with the fader, keeping the eighth notes constant in your record hand.

Half Notes and Whole Notes

Like the half rest, the half note receives two beats, or half of a bar in 4/4 time. Like the whole rest, a whole note will receive four counts or one whole bar in 4/4 time.

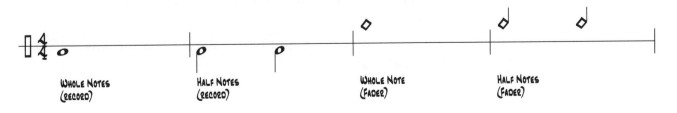

Fig. 11.5. Whole notes and half notes

Play along with exercises 27 to 32 on side 2, track 6.

■ **Exercise 27**

In this exercise, the record hand moves back and forth in continuous eighth notes, while the fader hand plays simple rhythms. This is a good way to start getting used to playing different rhythms with your two hands. When you have a rest in the fader hand, you won't be able to hear the scratches in your record hand, but keep playing those eighth notes anyway!

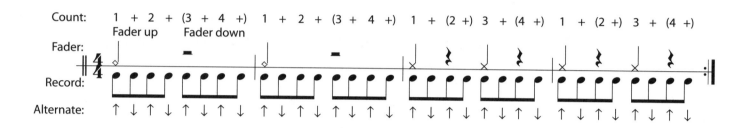

■ **Exercise 28**

When you turn up the fader for a single forward stroke, you will be essentially playing a stab. This exercise is really a combination of the stab and a continuous basic scratch.

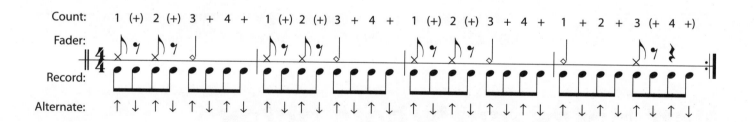

Dotted Rhythms

Adding a dot to a note will increase its value by one half.

Since a quarter note receives one beat, a **dotted quarter note** will receive one and a half beats.

Using the same formula, the **dotted half note** will receive three beats. The **dotted eighth note** will receive three-fourths of a beat. Use the chart below as a reference.

DOTTED NOTES

$$\text{♩.} = \text{♩} + \text{♪} = 1\ 1/2\ \text{BEATS}$$

$$\text{𝅗𝅥.} = \text{𝅗𝅥} + \text{♩} = 3\ \text{BEATS}$$

$$\text{♪.} = \text{♪} + \text{♬} = 3/4\ \text{BEAT}$$

Fig. 11.6. Dotted notes

■ **Exercise 29**

Now we'll add to the mix playing isolated backstrokes, which is the same technique as the back stab. The rhythm will be slightly more complex and syncopated, as well.

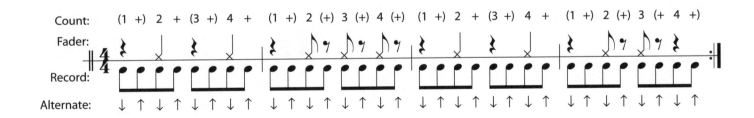

■ **Exercise 30**

This is a straight-ahead exercise with an emphasis on the downbeats.

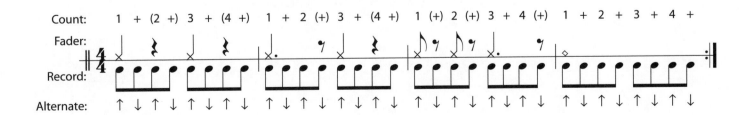

Drags

Drags are slow, drawn-out scratches. Drags last longer (typically half notes and whole notes) so you must move the record slowly, or you may run out of record to drag.

Fig. 11.7. Dragging the record

You can alter the sound of drags by changing the speed of your record hand, and by using different fader techniques. You can combine drags with faster rhythms in the fader to create a variety of effects.

■ **Exercise 31**

This exercise combines drags, stabs, and back stabs. The rhythms are pretty straightforward.

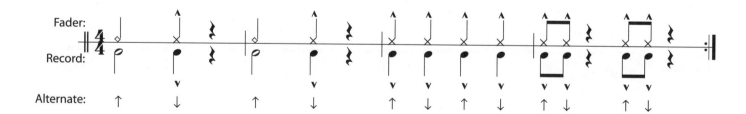

■ **Exercise 32**

In the first and third measures of this exercise, the fader hand cuts off sharply on the "and" of 2, and the "and" of 4. In the second measure, note the continuous eighth notes in the record hand.

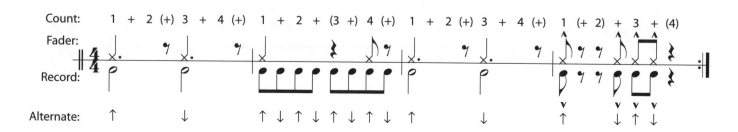

The Transformer

Play along with side 2, track 6.

■ **Exercise 33**

The **transformer** is essentially a combination of a slow drag in the record hand, with quick fader movement. Introduced in Philadelphia, this technique has been popularized by Jazzy Jeff and Cash Money.

You might want to go back over exercises 17 through 19 with your fader hand to warm up.

Here, we're using two-beat (half-note) drags in the record hand against eighth notes and eighth note triplets performed by the up-fader.

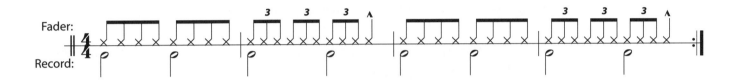

■ **Exercise 34**

Four-beat (whole-note) drags in the record hand mean that you must move nice and slowly so you don't run out of drag space. In the fader hand we actually break into sixteenth notes in the second and fourth bar. If this is too fast for your fader hand at first, slow down the record you're playing along with to a speed you can handle.

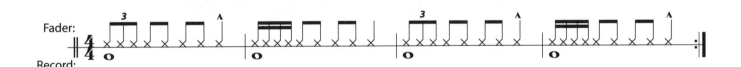

While you'll probably find it easier to execute the transformer with the crossfader, using the up-fader is a handy technique, as well.

Cutting

Cutting, also known as "forward," repeats a short sample of sound from a record, like a keyboardist uses a digital sampler. You can use any sound for cutting: a word, a phrase, a brass stab, a snare drum, a burst of noise, you name it!

The key to cutting is to keep track of exactly where the sound you're using begins on the record. Mark the location of the sample with an adhesive dot or cassette label. Visualize where your fingers need to catch the record in order to bring the sound back to the beginning.

To practice cutting, start with the "One!" at the top of side 1, track 1 of *Turntable Technique* (or use a short word at the beginning of another track). On the mixer, put the crossfader in the middle.

1. With the platter spinning, cue up the word "One!" and hold the record just before the sound.

Fig. 11.8. Holding the record

2. Set the record in motion, letting the sound ("One!") play, fader up.

Fig. 11.9. Playing the sample (hand is off the record)

3. Catch the record at the spot you were just holding onto, and quickly bring the fader all the way down.

Fig. 11.10. Catching the sample

4. Bring the record back to the starting point with the fader down.

Fig. 11.11. Bringing the sample back

5. Repeat steps 2 through 4, firing at will.

Cutting is similar to the stab, except that when you cut, you let the turntable play the sound, rather than pushing it forward yourself. As with the stab, it's important to mute the entire back scrape to keep your cuts clean and tight sounding.

Play along with exercises 35 through 38 on side 2, track 7.

■ **Exercise 35**   Cutting

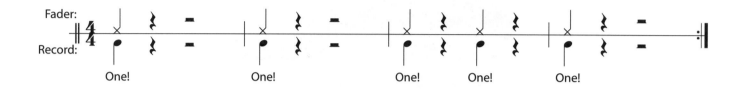

Half Note Triplets

Half note triplets split four beats (one entire bar) into three equal parts rather than two. You play three half note triplets in the same time as two half notes.

Half note triplets make a good rhythm for cutting because of their lazy, "back of the beat" feel.

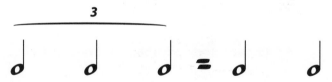

Fig. 11.12. Half note triplets

■ **Exercise 36**   Playing along with the record will help you get the half note triplets.

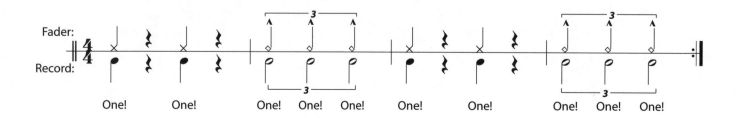

■ **Exercise 37**   This exercise is just straight quarter notes. Practice it to work on the accuracy and speed of your cutting.

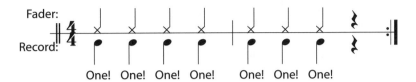

Ties

When you **tie** two notes together, you combine the amount of time given to each. Two eighth notes tied together equals one beat, since each eighth received half a beat in the first place.

One reason notes are tied is so we can hold a note over a bar line.

Fig. 11.13. Notes tied over the bar

We also tie notes that hold over the middle of the measure in 4/4 time, because it makes the rhythms easier to read and feel. (Trust me, it does — even if it seems weird at first.)

This concept is called the **imaginary bar line**, and it makes rhythms easier to handle. Just imagine there is a bar line before the third beat of the measure, and you'll be all set.

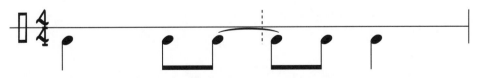

Fig. 11.14. Notes tied over the imaginary bar line

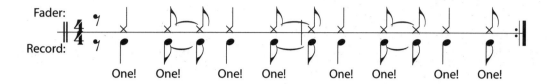

Don't let the way this exercise looks scare you; it's really simple. To play it, let the first eighth rest (half beat) go by, then think of playing quarter notes on all of the upbeats. Once you get used to playing on the upbeats, you'll want to do it a lot. It's much hipper than hanging out with the downbeats all the time!

After you get the hang of cutting, find tracks with different words and instruments to work into your routine. There are a lot of great records out there to use. The *Turntablist's Toolkit* is a great source for spoken words, sound effects, and unusual melodic material.

12. Using the Crossfader

It's probably safe to say that many beginning DJs go right for the crossfader, and ignore up-fader and switch technique until their crossfader chops are already established. Their facility on the switch and up-fader never comes close to their crossfader skill, so they wind up hardly ever using anything but the crossfader.

This is the main reason I've put off teaching crossfader technique until you've gotten some up-fader and switch experience under your belt. While the crossfader may be the most accessible single control on the DJ mixer, having the facility to move effortlessly between all of the controls opens up a whole world of possibilities, and will make you a much better player.

First, let's look at how the crossfader works.

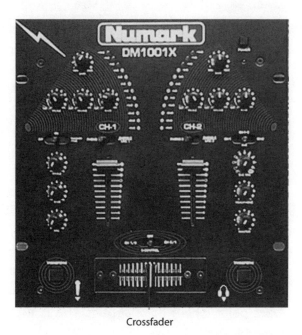

Crossfader

Fig. 12.1. Crossfader

Most crossfaders weren't designed to provide an even crossfade between the two channels. There is usually a large space in the middle of the range (about half the length of the crossfader) where both turntables are up to full volume. Many of the more advanced DJ mixers let you adjust the curve of the crossfader to suit your taste.

Locating the Cut-On Point

The **cut-on point** is the point where the sound from the opposite channel suddenly cuts on. While it varies from mixer to mixer, the cut-on point is usually about an eighth to a quarter of the way across the crossfader. It's important to know exactly where the cut-on point is for each of the channels serviced by your crossfader.

Fig 12.2. Locating the cut-on point

To get used to finding the cut-on point:

1. Play any record on the left turntable.

2. With the right hand, move the crossfader all the way to the right, killing the sound of the record.

3. Slowly move the crossfader to the left, until you can hear the sound of the left turntable clearly. Pay attention, both visually and by feel, to the exact point where this happens. This is the cut-on point for your left turntable.

4. Practice flicking the sound of the left turntable on and off, quickly moving the crossfader back and forth over the cut-on point.

Fig. 12.3. Playing the crossfader

Repeat the above steps, using the right turntable and your left hand to find the cut-on point for the right turntable.

Keep your movements as precise and efficient as possible. Don't go past the cut-on point any further than necessary.

Crossfader Technique

You can manipulate the crossfader simply by moving it back and forth. Or, you can play it precisely by using your fingers to attack each note, and your thumb to release them. "Think of your thumb as a spring," suggests QBert.

Here is a primer on basic crossfader technique:

1. Play any record on the left turntable.

2. Using your right hand, push the crossfader all the way over to the right with your thumb.

3. Let your thumb rest gently on the left side of the crossfader. Think of your thumb as a spring, and apply gentle pressure.

4. Allow your fingers to rear back a few inches, like a boxer winding up for a punch.

Fig. 12.4. Getting ready to strike

5. Attack the right side of the crossfader with your middle and ring fingers (or your index and middle fingers), pushing the fader over the cut-on point. Keep the pressure of your thumb constant, even though it is pushed back.

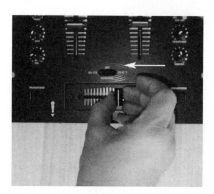

Fig. 12.5. Pushing the crossfader past the cut-on point

6. Release the pressure from your fingers, allowing your thumb to instantly push the crossfader all the way back over to the right.

Fig. 12.6. The thumb returning the crossfader to its original position

Steps 4 through 6 may be executed in a split second, depending on the length of the notes you are playing.

One-Handed Crossfader Practice

Cue up and let's play some white noise or a sustained tone on the left turntable. Play the following exercises using the crossfader. Switch hands (and turntables), and do it again.

Play along with exercises 39 through 45 using side 2, track 8.

■ **Exercise 39**

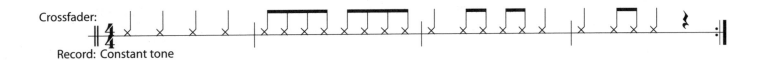

■ **Exercise 40**

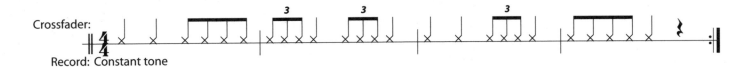

■ **Exercise 41**

This exercise adds staccato and legato articulations to indicate short and long notes.

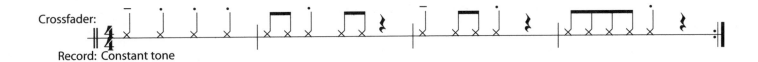

■ **Exercise 42**

By controlling exactly how far and fast you travel over the cut-on point, you can play accents using the crossfader.

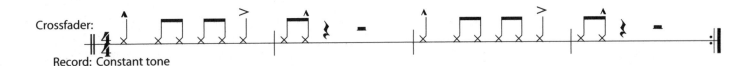

■ **Exercise 43**   This exercise works in some syncopation. Remember to count!

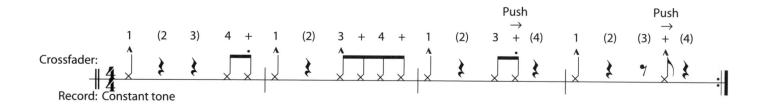

■ **Exercise 44**   Here we break into sixteenth notes. Slow the exercises down at first if you find the sixteenth notes too fast.

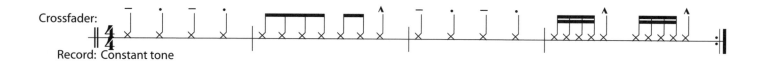

■ **Exercise 45**   This exercise explores the difference between eighth note triplets and sixteenth notes. Again, start slow and work up to speed.

For even more practice, go back and play through exercises 15 through 19 using the crossfader rather than the up-fader.

Two-Handed Scratching with the Crossfader

Ultimately, you want to be able to improvise intricate rhythms using both hands. The exercises in this section will help make that day come sooner.

Start by cueing up some white noise, a sustained tone, a spoken word, or a sound effect that lasts at least half a revolution, so you can scratch it back and forth continually.

Figure 12.7. Scratching using the crossfader

Play along with exercises 46 through 49 on side 2, track 9.

With your record hand, play quarter notes, alternating forward and backward strokes. With your crossfader hand, use the crossfader technique from earlier in this chapter to play the rhythms in the following exercises.

■ **Exercise 46**

This is a simple exercise designed to ease you into using the crossfader with the record hand.

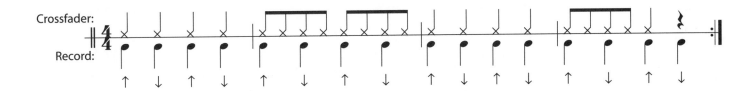

■ Exercise 47

This exercise repeats the same rhythm, but adds articulations. Listen to the difference on the companion record. Notice how the quarter notes turn into stabs and backstabs.

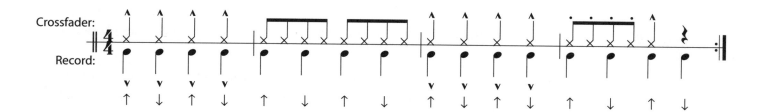

■ Exercise 48

Exercise 48 is syncopated, though you'll find the rhythm comes naturally once you get it. Remember to count out loud: "one-e-and-a, two-e-and-a, three-e-and-a, four-e-and-a." Listen to and play along with the record to make sure you've got it right.

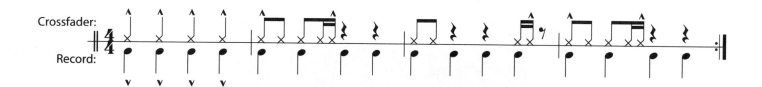

■ Exercise 49

In this exercise, the record hand moves slower, playing half note drags. The record hand breaks into a transformer with the sixteenth notes and eighth note triplets.

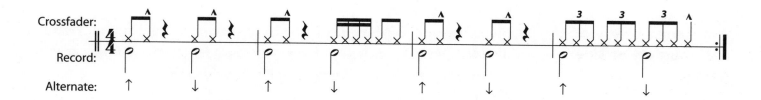

It's easy to substitute the crossfader for the up-fader or switch when performing the stabs, backstabs, transformers, and cutting exercises earlier in this book.

Go back now and **play exercises 22 through 38 using the crossfader**. I guarantee they will be much easier now than they were the first time!

The Crab

The crab sounds like a burst of rapid notes. Its name comes from how your fingers look as they fly over the crossfader—not unlike a crab running across the beach. Try clicking each of your fingers, in quick sequence, against your thumb, and you'll get the idea. QBert is often credited for popularizing this lightning-fast crossfader technique.

 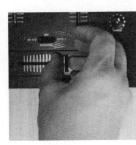 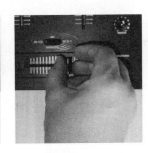  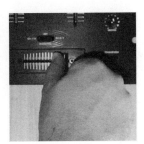

Figs. 12.8a–e. A four-finger crab

To perform the crab, your pinky, ring, middle, and index fingers force the crossfader over the cut-on point in rapid succession. Between each finger's attack, the thumb "springs" the crossfader back over the cut-on point to separate the notes.

Let's break the crab down so you can work on the dexterity of each finger.

We'll call your:

- index finger "i"

- middle finger "m"

- ring finger "r"

- pinkie "p"

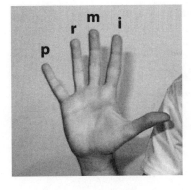

Fig. 12.9. Finger labels

Cue up some white noise or a continuous tone to scratch. Play the following exercises slowly at first, working up speed a little at a time. Resist the temptation to play fast and sloppy.

If you find it's too much at first to coordinate both hands, let the record play and concentrate on getting your individual fingers working accurately on the crossfader. Once you get each finger to attack and release cleanly, add the quarter-note movements with the record hand.

Play along with exercises 50–57 on side 2, track 10.

■ **Exercise 50**

Here we're using individual fingers on the crossfader, as described above. Make sure that your thumb forces the crossfader back over the cut-on point to make a clean break between each note.

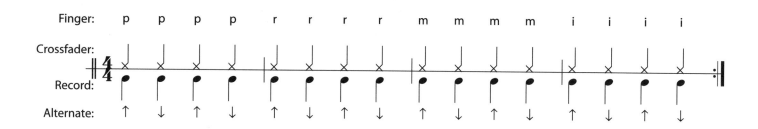

■ **Exercise 51**

Once you get comfortable using your fingers individually, speed things up a bit with the next exercise. Playing eighth notes with the individual fingers of your fader hand means that you'll have two attacks for each quarter-note move in the record hand. Don't hesitate to work your fader hand alone.

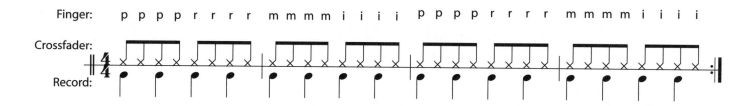

■ **Exercise 52**

In this exercise we'll move down to two attacks per finger in the fader hand rather than four. Work to make the attack with your pinkie just as strong as the attack with your index finger.

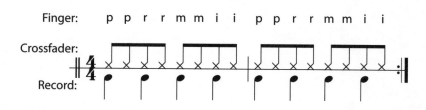

88

■ **Exercise 53**

Now we'll move to one attack per finger. Let the record play a continuous tone so you can concentrate on making your finger movements as precise as possible.

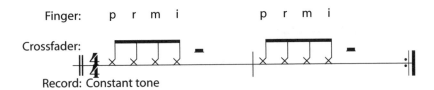

■ **Exercise 54**

Eighth note triplets speed up the finger movements a bit.

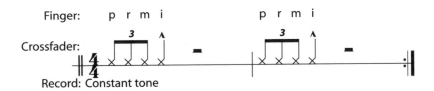

■ **Exercise 55**

Sixteenth notes speed things up a bit more.

■ **Exercise 56**

The crab doesn't always have to include all four fingers. Triplets work well played with the ring, index, and middle fingers. Since this should be a little easier than the sixteenth notes, try working in quarter-note record moves.

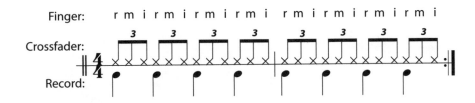

■ **Exercise 57**

Work up to this sixteenth note exercise slowly. Notice how this exercise repeats the index and middle fingers in quick sequence in the second measure.

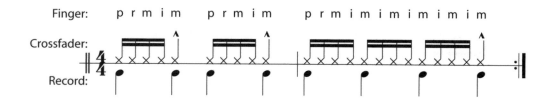

Play along with exercise 58 on side 2, track 11.

■ **Exercise 58**

This exercise uses the rhythm of the *William Tell Overture*. As always, practice both hands separately to master this piece of music.

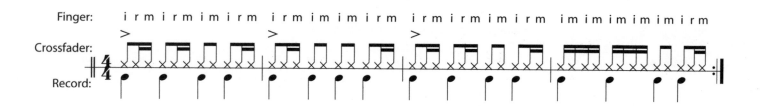

Don't rush getting your crab technique up to speed. Speed comes from familiarity with your material. The more often you practice, the faster you will become. Concentrate on playing as cleanly and accurately as possible.

13. Conclusion and Resources

While this is the first method book for the turntable so far, there are lots of other great resources you should know about. Most of them are accessible via the Internet. The site **www.toolsfordjs.com** will keep you up-to-date with what we have available at Berklee Press.

The DMC has lots of resources on their site at **www.dmcworld.com** including information on DMC battles, DJ pages, and an online store where you can buy their popular battle videos and lots of other DJ gear.

John Carluccio, Ethan Imboden, and Raymond Pirtle, Jr. have developed a very cool graphic way to write down turntable music. It's called TTM, for Turntable Transcription Methodology. Somewhat like tablature for the turntable, the system is very flexible and well thought out, though the developers insist it is a work in progress and invite input. You can check it out at **www.battlesounds.com**.

To keep abreast of QBert and the Invisibl Skratch Piklz, you can check out their site at **www.skratchpiklz.com**.

The site **www.hip-hop.com** has links to the ITF (International Turntablist Federation).

The site **www.turntablism.com** has lots of resources, including some online scratch tutorials by Bevan Jee, with scratch samples by Doc Rice.

And of course, **www.berkleepress.com** will be adding all sorts of resources as time goes on.

Although we've gone over a lot of material, this is just the beginning. There are many things we just don't have room to cover here. Intermediate scratching techniques such as the flare, the chirp, the orbit, and other large topic areas like beat juggling, hamster style, and melodic playing will have to wait for the next book.

Until then, practice well. *Stephen Webber*

PART 2.

Interviews

14. A Brief History

The term "DJ" has been around since the early days of radio. Although its meaning continues to evolve, DJ is short for "disc jockey," the name given to radio personalities who would switch records (jockey the discs), run the board, and introduce songs on the air.

Fig 13.1. The 1998 DMC Hall of Fame recipients: Grand Master Flash, Grand Wizard Theodore, and GrandMixer DXT. Not pictured is Afrika Bambaataa. Photo courtesy of DMC.

DJing (live, with turntables) is one of the four main expressions of what's come to be known as "hip-hop culture." The other three expressions of hip-hop culture are rap (MCing), graffiti art, and b-boying (known to the media as breakdancing). Hip-hop grew out of the street culture in the Bronx and around New York City in the late '70s.

One of the first DJs to rock the Bronx was a Jamaican known as Kool Herc. Herc played at block parties, parks, community centers, and clubs in the early- to mid-'70s. He assembled a strong following. In Jamaica, sound-system battles were a big part of the reggae scene. DJ Kool Herc built up a massive sound system that put the competition in the Bronx to shame. His choice of records—obscure funk, soul, and r&b—was very influential to the growing scene.

DJ Kool Herc also pioneered the art of the break. When Herc noticed that the b-boys would save their best moves for certain parts of the record (often the drum break), he set out to extend that portion of the track. By using two identical copies of the same record, Kool Herc would repeat the break as many times as he wanted by switching between the turntables.

Herc influenced many young DJs in the Bronx, including a young electronics student named Joseph Saddler, later to be known as Grand Master Flash. Grand Master Flash perfected the technique of seamlessly repeating the best part of a record by "cutting" between two identical copies, one on each turntable.

Through techniques such as the "back door" and the "backspin/clock theory," Flash was able to pinpoint the break with great accuracy. His background in electronics helped him design his own cue system (which he called the "peek-a-boo system"), so he could use headphones to cue up the exact part of a record before the audience could hear it. Grand Master Flash, with his crew of MCs, the Furious Five, is responsible for making some momentous records, including "Freedom" and "The Message."

Afrika Bambaataa, known as the "Godfather of Hip Hop," also made ground-breaking records, including the electro-funk hit, "Planet Rock." Bambaataa was already well known around New York as an influential DJ and as the founder of an organization named the Universal Zulu Nation.

In the book *Rap Attack*, by David Toop, Bambaataa describes some of the mixing he did in the Bronx back in the early- to mid-'80s.

> I used to like to catch the people who'd say, "I don't like rock. I don't like Latin." I'd throw on Mick Jagger—you'd see the blacks and the Spanish just throwing down, dancing crazy. I'd say, "I thought you said you didn't like rock." They'd say, "Get out of here." I'd say, "Well, you just danced to the Rolling Stones." "You're kidding!"
>
> I'd throw on "Sergeant Pepper's Lonely Hearts Club Band"—just that drum part—one, two, three, BAM! and they'd be screaming and partying. I'd throw on The Monkees, "Mary Mary"—just the beat part where they'd go "Mary, Mary, where are you going?"—and they'd start going crazy. I'd say, "You just danced to The Monkees." They'd say, "You liar. I didn't dance to no Monkees." I'd like to catch people who categorize records.

Grand Wizard Theodore was just a little kid when Grand Master Flash started to feature him at gigs. Theodore had to stand on a milk crate to reach the turntables. He amazed Flash and the audience, repeating the breaks on records by accurately lifting the needle and putting it back down earlier in the track. Later, Theodore began to use the sound of the record being moved back and forth while the needle is in the grooves as a musical device—a practice now known by DJs everywhere as "scratching."

In the meantime, Grand Mixer DST—who has since changed his name to Grand Mixer DXT—was taking it all in. His skill on the turntables eventually attracted the attention of jazz legend Herbie Hancock, who featured DST on the turntables in his hit-making band in the '80s. DST's appearances on television, scratching on Hancock's "Rockit," sent kids across America scrambling to their parents' turntables to experiment with this new art form.

Turntable Competitions

In the '80s, Tony and Christine Prince founded the Disco Mix Club (DMC) in the UK. The DMC was meant to be a mixing battle for house DJs. However, DJ Cheese from Plainfield, New Jersey changed everything at the 1986 DMC world finals, when he included scratching in his winning routine.

Fig. 13.2. The X-ecutioners, Rob Swift, Total Eclipse, Roc Raida, and Mista Sinista, are one of the most innovative DJ crews on the East Coast. Photo by Karen Miller.

In 1987, the DMC began putting the finals out on video, a practice that continues to this day. Competition, and the chance for new DJs to scope out the top competitor's techniques on video, has helped the art form evolve quickly. DJs have innovated new scratches, beat juggles, melody playing, and body tricks in their routines to stay a step ahead of the competition.

Another significant contribution of the DMC competition is the popularization of DJ crews. In 1992, the Rocksteady DJs (a trio of QBert, MixMaster Mike, and Apollo) took the world championship and provided a preview of what would become the Invisibl Skratch Piklz.

The Bullet Proof Scratch Hamsters, The Fifth Platoon, the Beat Junkies, and the X-men (later, the X-ecutioners) furthered the cause of turntable ensembles. In 1999, the DMC/Vestax/Numark Team Battle was added to the DMC's roster of events.

Christie Z-Pabon became the U.S. Events Coordinator for the DMC in late 1997. Christie, a long time hip-hop enthusiast, has worked to make judging more consistent and improve the quality of the popular videos. She has brought hip-hop back to center stage at DMC events.

Fig. 13.3. The DMC's Christie Z-Pabon and X-ecutioner Roc Raida. Photo by Tony Prince.

"We now have b-boys, b-girls, poppers, and/or lockers performing," reports Z-Pabon. "We have a graf artist that we try to use often for all of our literature, and we try to bring in different DJs to showcase in order to show all of the different ways a person can DJ. There is no one recipe."

The field continues to expand. The International Turntablist Federation began holding its own world championships in the mid-'90s. There are many other competitions as well, with more coming on the scene each year.

DJs are turning up in recording studios as instrumentalists, recording artists (with or without MCs), and producers. Stylistically and creatively, the turntable's horizons continue to expand.

15. DJ QBert

From Champion to Soul Searcher

Fig. 14.1. DJ QBert. Photo by Eugene Pae, ©1998.

DJ QBert is the top pickle. Through a combination of amazing talent, perpetual energy, and a skewed but endearing sense of humor, he owns the vibrant San Francisco DJ scene the way a kid owns Christmas morning. Born Richard Quitevis, QBert has been called "the Jimi Hendrix and Eddie Van Halen of the turntable."

In the early '90s, QBert won DMC championships both as a solo DJ and with his crewmates, MixMaster Mike and Apollo. The team DJ sets they turned in laid the groundwork for DJ crews to follow.

Along with the rest of his crew, The Invisibl Skratch Piklz, QBert has cranked out several videos. The primitively shot (but incredibly entertaining) *Turntable TV* keeps DJ fans abreast of everything Piklz, and shares tips and tricks with the faithful.

Cuts from QBert's innovative album, *Wave Twisters*, are being turned into an animated film. He's in high demand for concerts all over the world.

Despite his busy schedule, QBert is dedicated to educational efforts. QBert presents many turntable workshops, and the ISP have set up the Global Skratch Foundation, to help students who want to advance the art of turntabling.

As we talked recently, animators were gathering at his house to talk about their upcoming projects.

How important is a sense of humor to what you do?

I've always thought that the DJ community is a little too serious. Art is entertainment, and you know, there's fun in that!

To get that whole creative energy, it's like being a kid again. I've always been searching for a kid's sense of creativity. Like, for instance, a lawyer could spend his whole life learning how to be a lawyer, but a kid will just totally win the whole argument. "No! You've got boogers on your nose and you *are* a dork!"

You credit Miles, Monk, Hendrix, and Les Paul as your influences. What did you get from each of them?

From Miles and Thelonius Monk I got silence, and the poetry of it all, and the lyric quality of their style.

From Jimi Hendrix, that whole zone, just blowing and letting the universe speak through you. And all the tricks—Jimi Hendrix had all these tricks! Different ways of expressing himself. It's like each trick that you learn is a new word in your vocabulary of music, so the more tricks you know, the more you can speak articulately through your music.

Les Paul is like a total innovator. He's an inspiration, as we're designing mixers and turntables for the future of DJing and scratching. Inventing things. And the way Les Paul plays, too. He's very funny and totally natural.

There're all sorts of things that each artist has to offer. Every time I watch a video, I'll see something new, and I'll say, "Oh, I didn't trip off that last time, but check this out."

How much do you practice?

I try to practice at least a little bit every day. Before a gig, I'll practice at least two whole days. Pretty much all day for two days. When I'm doing all these other projects, I have to cut out two days before a show and make sure I have turntables in the hotel room before the performance.

If I don't have a show coming up, I won't always practice every day if I'm not feeling it. Sometimes being away from it is actually an advantage, because when you get to it, it's like, "Whoa!" You're kind of fresh. Your drive is there.

Can you describe the difference in energy between playing solo and playing with a crew?

When you're with an ensemble, it's like you're a team. Everyone works as a crew and puts in a team effort, so it sounds great. I guess I got this from some football player—he said, "There's no 'I' in 'team.'" Everyone's helping each other, it's one beautiful piece. When you go solo, the advantage is that you can totally express yourself, as the "I." They're both good.

When you're playing with a band, it's like you're another musical instrument in the band, but with all turntables, it's like you're every instrument. You can jump to drums, then you can jump to guitar, then you can jump to bass, then you can jump to farts, jump to chicken squeaking, whatever. So everyone is whatever instrument they choose to be at a given time.

Fig. 14.2. The Invisibl Skratch Picklz, from left to right: MixMaster Mike, D-Styles, Qbert, Yogafrog, Shortkut. Photo by Karen Miller, © 1997.

When you're playing with the Invisibl Skratch Picklz, how much is planned out, and how?

Sometimes we'll write out stuff and we'll have like a diagram of where to go here, and you improvise here and I'll improvise there, and we'll have like a set chorus here, or wherever the bridge is, blah blah blah.

Other times we'll just go into a show where 100 percent will be freestyle. And while we're scratching we'll say, "Okay, grab the drums! Go solo! Go do a routine! Grab a beat!"

Do you have any formal musical background?

I went to school and I learned a bit about reading music. I mostly learned about drumming and patterns. My style of scratching is pretty percussive.

What techniques have you contributed to the art form?

I guess I'm known for the crab scratch, which is where you use all your fingers across the fader. Basically, it's like you're snapping all your fingers. Like when you snap a finger, but you snap all of them. Just snap them on the side of the fader, and use your thumb as a spring.

What inspired you to get into DJing?

I guess around '85 or '84, there was a song called "Rockit," and there was "Buffalo Gals," and they had scratching. I seen 'em on TV, which was what really tripped me, and I was like "Whoa, what's that?" I was thirteen or fourteen. I started when I was fifteen, that was like in '85.

Can you remember what it felt like to win the '91 DMC US Finals?

I couldn't believe it. I thought, "Am I just lucky here?" I think that maybe all the good competitors must have been home sleeping or something. Maybe they didn't want to enter this year and they gave me a chance, so I was like real happy about that.

It would kind of get to my head sometimes. "Okay, yeah I'm like really good." But then I'll go home and hear all these other DJs that never compete. They're called "bedroom DJs." They just stay home. And they'll just kick my ass any day of the week. They just do it for the love of it, rather than competing. We call them "soul searchers."

They have surfers like that in Hawaii. There're the professional guys that compete, and then there're the soul searchers who can do everything. They can surf from one island to another island, and they don't even compete. I mean a champion can be equally as good as a soul searcher, it's just that a soul searcher doesn't compete. It's crazy.

What does the future hold for playing the turntable?

It grows every day. Every day it evolves more and more. People are using different sounds and developing new techniques. That infinity of sounds times that infinity of techniques is like infinity times infinity, forever.

16. DJ Swamp

Playin' in the Band

Fig. 15.1. DJ Swamp (right) and the author at Berklee College of Music. Photo by Tim Lyons.

DJ Swamp is making history everywhere he goes. The first DJ to ever present a clinic at Berklee, Swamp visited the campus between shows with Grammy-award-winning artist Beck at Boston's Orpheum theater.

Swamp has been a DJ since the '80s, and has no less than seven double albums of break beats and "skip-proof" scratch tools records to his name. His outrageous skills on the turntables have flabbergasted audiences around the world, and won him the 1996 United States DMC Championship.

Since moving to L.A. to take the gig with Beck, he's also been doing lots of studio work as a session turntablist. By now, Swamp has scratched on so many records and movie soundtracks that if you live on the planet, you've probably heard him play.

While touring the world with Beck, Swamp is able to keep working on remixes for numerous high-profile clients, as well as his own projects with his Pro Tools–equipped PowerBook.

Here's our conversation.

Did you play in other bands before the Beck gig?

I was in a band called Nation of Teflon Souls with Stefanie Eulinberg, who's now Kid Rock's drummer.

How did you get the gig with Beck?

I had sent tapes to the Dust Brothers, and I think that's how he first heard about me. Then I went to a show in Ohio and I took him a tape. I didn't get to see him, but I gave it to his manager.

Then I was DJing a rave, and somebody had brought a copy of *SPIN* and was like, "Beck mentioned your name. " I was just like, "What?" And then a couple days later he called me and we went on tour.

What's the collaboration process like with you and Beck in the studio?

I show up, Beck says "Do this," then I go home. Pretty much all there is to it.

He has a pretty good idea of what he wants?

Yeah, completely. Specific sounds. He likes . . . like, weird space noises.

How do you hear yourself on stage playing with Beck?

We've got really good "in-ears," [in-ear monitors] they're real expensive. I think that us and In Sync are the only ones that use them! [Laughs] They work great.

Tell me about your skip-proof records.

I made the skip-proof records so you could scratch a lot harder. They only have like three samples per side. Also, if you play with a band, guitar players jump around a lot, so your records would skip. They've done decent enough so I can keep putting out new volumes and that sort of thing. I don't really make 'em to make money, I make 'em for me to use.

What break-beat records do you have out?

Skip-Proof Scratch Tools, volumes 1 through 3, *Never-Ending Break Beats*, volumes 1 and 2, *Wax Craft*, and *Swamp Breaks*.

How do you set your tone arm weights?

I put them in backwards, not all the way up, but in the gap when you hear them click. Then I set them to "4."

Where do you mark your records?

At the on/off switch light.

What else would you like to do in your career?

Produce a whole slew of groups. I've done a lot of remixes for people. As far as producing, I've just now gotten my first real producing job, and that's producing a song for Kelly Ali. She was the singer in the Sneaker Pimps. I'm working on it now. She wrote the words, I wrote the music.

Tell me about the remixes you've done.

I've done remixes for Bloodhound Gang, Morcheeba, a couple of Japanese groups like Zilch and Fantastic Plastic Machine, and a pretty popular Pakistani artist.

Sometimes, they just want a better beat added. Sometimes they'll just let you go, "Just make it as weird as possible." They usually give 'em to me on ADAT. I usually do it at home. I do it all internally in the computer.

What projects have you played on as a session turntablist?

Besides Beck, I did some stuff on Kid Rock, Crystal Method, Morcheeba, did the Dandy Warhols, Hansen. I worked with the Dust Brothers. The remixed theme from the X-Files, I did the scratching on that.

Are there turntablists in the musician's union in L.A. now?

Yeah, now there is. It didn't happen until a few years ago, though. In order to get paid through the union, a lot of times [I'd have to] say I was an engineer, or if I was performing live, I'd say I was a dancer. If you were getting a work permit out of the country, it made it a lot easier if you just said you were something else. I think they've changed now.

Advice for up-and-coming DJs?

You've got to work, it's not just going to come to you. It really doesn't work like that. You've gotta do the work.

17. MixMaster Mike

B-Boy Becomes Beastie

Fig. 16.1. MixMaster Mike. Photo by Karen Miller, ©1997.

MixMaster Mike got into hip-hop through b-boying back in 1984, when he was fourteen years old. He started trying to mix with two old cassette decks from his uncle's storage room, using the pause buttons to match beats.

His life was changed forever when he saw Grand Mixer DST (now DXT) scratching on TV with Herbie Hancock. Soon, Mike was in the mobile DJ business, playing everything from weddings to garage parties.

After showing a young Richard Quitevis (DJ QBert) the basics of scratching, a rivalry developed. Mike even challenged QBert to a battle in Q's own school cafeteria. After QBert won the U.S. DMC championship in Chicago, MixMaster Mike entered the Superman Battle for World Supremacy in New York City and became the first West-Coast DJ to win.

In 1992, the two decided to put their rivalry behind them and form a DJ trio with Apollo, which took the DMC World Championship. In 1993, Mike and Q-Bert took the crown again as a duo. The following year, they laid down their swords and helped judge the competition.

Mike was a founding member of the Invisibl Skratch Piklz. His record, *Anti-Theft Device*, has drawn rave reviews. Recently, MixMaster Mike has been recording and touring with the Beastie Boys.

You were inspired by Grand Mixer DXT?

When I was a kid, I'd seen him perform with Herbie Hancock and it really, really inspired me, seeing him on the turntables. We [the Skratch Piklz] got to do a show with him in Poland with Bill Laswel, and it was pretty overwhelming.

Describe to me this DJ battle in QBert's school cafeteria.

Oh, man. [Laughs] Okay. . . Actually, it was a battle between me and him. We both had our own mobile DJ groups. We set up our own light shows and stuff, and had our own home speakers. I set my rig up on one side and he set his rig up on the other side. And me and him just went at it, back and forth.

Like he'd go on for twenty minutes and then I'd go on for twenty minutes. The crowd would come my way, then the crowd would go his way, then the crowd would come my way. . . . It was all crowd response. And actually, there was really no winner. Nobody could tell who the winner was, because it was just like a back-and-forth, back-and-forth kind of thing.

I can recall QBert coming over to my house, and me showing him the first steps of scratching. I used to do garage parties around the way, and he used to come around and just watch me scratch. Like I would see him at every garage party I'd do. I'd think, "There goes that kid again. He's right there lookin' at me." Finally I gave him my number. He told me he was going to come over and check me out. So he used to come over my house, and I used to show him like the first scratch steps, you know?

Did he pick it up pretty fast?

Oh, yeah, he did. He kinda like took it and just ran off with it, boy. And he turned into a monster.

Do you still judge DJ battles?

Actually, right now, it just became so hectic for me to judge anything. Plus I don't feel like I'm here to judge anybody now, because everybody's got their own particular style.

I've just moved on to taking this turntable art worldwide, flying all over the place, whether it be with the Beasties or just my shows. Taking this art further, you know what I mean? Planting seeds everywhere I go.

What do you look for in young players and what do you appreciate in other people's playing?

Sound, just the way they sound. And of course their technique. And what music and sounds they pick. I can tell [from] what the turntablist used, I can tell their musical background. Whether they use rock or hip-hop or whatever.

I look to see if they use records that I don't know, 'cause most of the kids use all the same records all the time. The same battle breaks, our break records or someone else's break records. I can just tell that they're pretty much just remixing those same break records. Then you can't really tell the DJs apart, because they all sound the same, because they're all using the same records. I like to see someone just break out with their own stuff, you know what I mean?

What's it like working with the Beastie Boys?

I open up for the Beasties. I do the first 20 minutes of their concert. You just never know when you walk onto the stage in these stadiums how many people there're gonna be. I've played in front of like 50,000 to 150,000 people in an arena. You walk up there and it's just total energy. I mean, talk about a rush. You can feel the energy out there.

The PA system is so loud that when you scratch you can feel it on your feet. It's just tremendous. It's helped me out a lot. I don't get stage fright anymore. I don't get that nervousness in my stomach, where I used to go out, and was like, "Oh no." Now I don't care who's out there or how many people are out there, 'cause I've seen a sea of people.

It's been a great experience though, 'cause being with the Beastie Boys allowed me to take this art like world-, WORLDwide. To kids out in Scotland and Barcelona, Spain, takin' this turntable art just all over the world. So much satisfaction, ya know?

Tell me about the Korn remix you did.

[Laughs] Oh, man! That was somethin' I whipped up so fast. My old manager requested that I do it.

I was in the middle of leaving on tour with the Beasties. So, I got this DAT of a demo from Korn, and I'm just like "Whoa, I'll try to do the best I can in a day." The DAT had all the tracks separately, all these pieces of music one after the other. I'd never heard the song before. Basically, I just scratched some beats, and did a little this-and-that over it.

To tell you the truth, I don't know how it came out, but I'm responsible for that Korn remix. And now they're huge, you know? I got that Korn DAT a long, long time ago, at the end of 1997. Way before they blew up.

I put it together on a DA38 TASCAM multitrack digital recorder.

Both *Vibe* and *Entertainment Weekly* have compared you to the guitarist Jimmie Page, what do you make of that?

I really don't understand that quote. It's interesting. I'm very familiar with Jimmie Page, but I don't really get the comparison. I'm more into musicians like Miles Davis. Who knows?

What do you feel like you've contributed to the art of turntabling?

Having a more improvisational sound. Not so robotically routined. More based upon just grabbing two pieces of vinyl and manipulating it on the spot. Not so robotic, more free-flow solo player.

I'm actually responsible for playing the drums on the turntable. Not just letting drums play, but playing the kick and the snare in real time. As a band, QBert, Apollo, and I were responsible for actually making the turntable into different instruments. Picking up guitar strums and actually playing them as a guitar. Picking up flute and horns. Playing the saxophone and scratching a sax so it actually sounds like a saxophone.

What kind of material do you look for on vinyl?

Instruments by themselves and nice long streaks of noise.

Any advice for new players?

I'd like to tell other DJs who are getting starting to brush up on their musical history. I know kids these days are deprived in what they grow up listening to, because there're not too many bands that are out who are really, really influential.

Back in the day, I used to listen to Jimi Hendrix, Coltrane, and Miles Davis. Get into wide ranges of different music, that's what helped me out a lot, listening to different players. Blues even just helped me a lot, just broadened my musical horizons and gave me a wider perspective on where I wanted to go with my art.

Where do you see turntable art going in the next millennium?

Hopefully, me and Q can take it to Carnegie Hall. For now, we're going to put out some records, put out some music.

18. DJ A-Trak

Prodigy from the North

Fig. 17.1. DJ A-Trak. Photo courtesy of DMC.

A-Trak isn't your typical world-champion battle DJ. He's from Canada. When he won his first world title, he had only been DJing for two years. He was barely old enough to drive. He's an excellent student, juggling not only beats but serious amounts of studying as well. I interviewed A-Trak on a rare school night when he didn't have homework.

Do you call yourself a "DJ" or a "turntablist"?

Both. I try not to pay too much attention to all the terminology. When the term "turntablist" came out, people were paying more attention to the term itself than to what the DJs were really doing. People would make a point out of calling themselves turntablists and not DJs, and it started getting annoying to me after a while. The basic difference, I think, is that the DJ is more the overall entertainer, whereas the turntablist is more the musician: manipulating the records to recreate your own music. I'm a battle DJ, I'm a turntablist, I'm also a bit of just a regular DJ, I guess, if I find myself just spinning records.

Do you play for parties or shows?

I do shows, I play at parties. I travel for shows. I don't do parties where I'll just spin. I'm always booked to do showcases, then once in a while I'll also spin, but the main thing is showcasing my routines. When I play live, I don't usually go past 10 minutes nonstop, 'cause it can get a bit heavy for the crowd, I think, if it's really technical. So, I'll do one or two sets like that.

What goes into planning a good routine?

I think it's really a combination of lots and lots of different factors. If we're talking about a beat juggle, the most important factor is if it sounds good, if it's entertaining, and sounds nice to listen to in a club or on a loud system. Then there're the technical aspects, like are the tricks technical and varied? There's the originality aspect, like is it too similar to what other people are doing or is it in a category of its own?

Transitions between patterns, I don't think there's a formula. It's just a question of finding a way not to break the tempo too abruptly and to kind of mix the songs slow, one into the other. And then, if you're looking at an overall routine, I appreciate seeing beat juggling as much as scratching. Not necessarily the same quantity, but if I see someone do nothing but beat juggles in a showcase, I think, "Okay, but what about his scratch?" If I see someone just scratch the beat for 10 minutes, I'll be like, "Alright, but can he organize that into a scratch routine? Can he juggle at all?" I think it's a combination of all that.

What titles have you won?

First, I won the 1997 Technics/DMC World Championships. This year, I won the 1999 ITF World Championships, then in December, I won the Vestax Extravaganza World Finals, in Tokyo.

How long have you been DJing?

I started in '95.

Did you teach yourself?

I taught myself, mostly. I practice by myself the big majority of the time. But that also means watching battle videos, and listening to scratches on albums and trying to figure them out. And once in a while, meeting up with other DJs and comparing tricks. But then the main practicing aspect is by myself in the basement.

What are you working on now?

For beat juggles, I just always try to come up with new juggles and use different kinds of records every time, and try to incorporate original patterns every time. But there's no specific path I'm following. And for scratches, I always try to make my scratches cleaner, and work on different combinations. I make up as many patterns as I can and work on the flow, which is the sound, and the way my scratches sound to the beat.

I'm doing some recording, also. I'm going to start working on an album pretty soon. I put out a seven-inch with Stone's Throw Records, in San Francisco. So, I'll be trying to work on more songs. Mostly like turntable songs. I record on eight tracks, and just layer stuff to make up songs. I have an ADAT now.

What do you look for in a piece to beat juggle?

The different sounds have to be separable. You can't really use a beat that's messy, because once you start breaking down that beat, people won't really understand what you're using. I usually look for like a choppy beat. And a beat that has room to work with, but that has a lot of sounds that I could switch up at the same time. If possible, on one hand, strong drums, but on the other hand, some melodies and samples I could use over the rhythm, also. I try to use different types of songs every time I do a juggle. Whatever sounds good and leaves me room to be creative.

What do you wish you could find on records that you haven't been able to?

When I record stuff, especially if I scratch over a song and I try to put together sentences, I'm always looking for the most insignificant words. Like "the" and "a" and "with." Just little link words. If you want to make a sentence out of different samples, it's easy to find actual words, but then to link the words together, it's hard to find.

Who inspired you to take up DJing?

I always listened to music with my brother, and we were listening to more rap records, so I'd be hearing some more scratches in songs. I remember a couple of times my brother would try to scratch. My father had a turntable, you know, for listening purposes. I'd seen my brother, with his friends, try to catch a snare on the beat and try to scratch it a bit. Once I was home by myself, like after school, and I just tried it.

This is without a slip mat?

Without a slip mat, it was without a crossfader for sure.

Did it mess up your dad's turntable or anything?

[Sheepishly] I might have broken a few needles . . . but it was worth it.

What did your parents think when you started getting into scratching?

They didn't really understand. When I told my father that I wanted to buy a used 1200 turntable, he didn't get it. He was like, "No. I'm not going to let you waste money on that. We already have a turntable!" I said, "Yeah, but I wanna scratch!" "What are you talking about? What do you know about scratching? What is this stuff?" I said, "You don't know, but I've been scratching!"

It took a lot of convincing. After that I just bought myself that used 1200 that I found. And then a little mixer. And when I saved up some more money, I bought myself a second turntable. And when time flew by, I guess my parents saw that this was real important for me. And when I started winning competitions, then they really understood.

What was the first competition that you entered?

The first competition I entered was the DMC that I ended up winning. My mother came to the world finals in Italy, but they weren't at the Montreal eliminations or the Canadian Finals—the Montreal Eliminations of '97. DMC's was the first battle I ever did.

And you won it.

Yeah, I remember coming home and my mom was up, 'cause she was nervous. And I said, "Yeah, I won."

I think that was a crucial moment in my parents' understanding that this could take me somewhere. I knew I had a shot at placing among the first three in Montreal, but I didn't see myself as a world-class DJ at all.

When you win the Canadian finals, for example, then the Canadian branch of the ITF or the DMC pays the champion's way to represent their county in the world finals.

So you're how old now?

Eighteen.

And you're flying to Japan and Honolulu and Italy to do all these competitions. What do the other kids at your high school think?

They're very confused, I think.

Do you perform at school?

I've done like one performance last year. I think they liked it. They were confused, though. I think people were impressed. But just on a day-to-day basis, my classmates just kinda forget that I have this whole other world outside of the school realm. The other day, I showed up at school with a copy of *Urb* magazine, with me on the cover, and they were like, "What are you doing there?"

How much do you practice?

I try to practice every day after school and stuff. I get in two to four hours a day, usually. This year, there's one day a week where I finish school at six, and then by the time I get home I barely have an hour before supper to scratch, and then I have homework to do. So, most of the time there's one day a week where I don't get to practice, but that's just these past few months. But overall, I practice daily. Usually, like three hours.

Do you have a specific practice routine?

I've seen DJs who actually have like warm-up exercises, the same as piano or whatever. But I have this little gadget called the "Grip-Master," which is like a finger exerciser with springs that each finger can control individually. I think it's meant for trumpet players or guitar players. I warm up with that a bit, just to wake up my fingers, and then I just start scratching.

Do you do a lot of work with individual fingers against the crossfader?

Yeah. Most of the movements are done with either the wrist or finger movements, but there're scratches like the crab that employ movements with one finger after the other. But actually most scratches that I do are either finger movements, with my forefinger and middle finger grouped together as one big finger, or wrist movements.

Do you use the pinkie for your crabs?

Sometimes. Most DJs just use the three—the forefinger, middle, and ring finger—but I use the pinkie sometimes.

Do you play any other instruments? Do you read music?

I've played piano before. Actually, I've been developing a notation system for scratching. I write down scratches.

I hear you're a pretty good student.

Yeah. Try to keep the grades up.

Christie (from DMC) says you get all A's. Is that true?

Yeah. I mean it doesn't work with A's or whatever. [He's in Canada.] Right now, I'm in what's called "CEGEP," which is between high school and university. But if you count the years, this is my twelfth year, so I'd be like a senior in the U.S. But here I have one more year and then I go into University. Now I'm studying sciences, more hours of physics and chemistry and biology and math, and less hours of English and French and history and stuff.

You're a Renaissance man.

[Long pause] You could say that.

Are you planning on DJing as a career, or doing something else and DJing as an artistic pursuit on the side?

I'm planning on pursuing my studies, but I'm also planning on continuing my DJ career. So I'm not really counting on DJing to be my main career throughout my life. I'm just going to keep doing it and keep going to school, and make sure I can do both at the same time.

See, it's tough for me to tell where this is going to take me, right now. I'm just thinking on a yearly basis, like, right now I'm in school and I'm DJing. I can't think too much in advance because it's unpredictable.

So how much homework do you have per night?

Tonight, miraculously, I have none, but that's the exception. Usually I have like two hours.

Do you have DJ friends there in Montreal?

I do, but they're a lot older. Not at my school. I am sure there are some DJs my age in Montreal, but I don't know them. In my school, there's not, though.

Who are your favorite DJs?

I have a lot. The X-ecutioners, the Skratch Piklz, Babu and Melo-d, Craze.
I think that pretty much sums it up.

Are there any techniques you've made up?

I didn't make up any one scratch really that stands by itself, but I've
made up some patterns, like combos of scratches, that already exist but
I'll do them in such a way that's my own.

19. DJ Craze

Nice Guys Finish First

Fig. 18.1. DJ Craze. Photo by Andrea Rapp, courtesy of DMC.

Arist Delgado, AKA DJ Craze, was born in Nicaragua on November 19, 1977. He moved to San Francisco with his folks a few years later, before settling in Miami.

Craze has taken the battle-DJ world by storm over the last few years, taking national and international titles seemingly at will. His career is currently at a whirlwind pace. I caught up with him at the elegant Elliot Hotel in Boston, the morning after a performance that kept him and his crew up until 4 a.m.

How did you get into DJing?

> I was fourteen when I started. My brother had equipment, he had Gemini 1800s. I would have to stay at his place after school every day so my mom could pick me up, and I'd scratch. When my brother moved out, I learned from watching videos. It took an eternity, because nobody was there to teach me. It was straight-up just me, by myself, watching the videos and trying to come up with stuff.

What was the first battle you entered?

The first battle that I entered was the Battle of Miami. I was fifteen years old, and I went up against this kid named Finger Prince. I wasn't even old enough to get into the club, and back then, nobody knew me. When they saw me go on stage, everyone was like, "Who is this little moron? Booooo!"

I got up and started dissin' right away. I started going through my battle routine records, I just freaked out. Everyone was like, "What? This fifteen-year-old kid is dissin' like a crazy!" I didn't even beat the guy. It's just that I was dissin' him so much that everybody was like, "Yeahhhh!!!"

I just kept joining battles anywhere I could. Then I hooked up with this dude who was like, "Yo, I'll fly you to New York to battle." I was a little Miami boy, so I was like, "Damn. I don't wanna got to New York and battle. I'll get f—-d up." But he was like, "Yo, just give it a shot." So I was like, "Alright, cool." So in '95 I came up there and joined the Zulu Nation Battle.

How did you do in the Zulu Nation Battle?

I won. They were like, "What the hell? [laughs] Who's this little Miami kid?" Back then I was going through puberty, so I had mad pimples and I just looked geeky. It was like, "Damn. Who is this guy?"

Do you think age might have helped you?

It helped for the first couple of battles, but for the Zulu Nation stuff, the people didn't care. They were just like, "If you're dope, you're dope." If you're young, people already have something to dis you about. So, they're just waiting for you to mess up. You just gotta keep it under control.

You've won the DMC World Championship for the last two years in a row. How has that affected your career?

Oh, that's been my career. That made my career. Before that, I was just doing gigs here and there, but it was nothing crazy, like now. Now it's crazy. Promoters all over the world would book you for being a DMC champion. They don't really care what you do. They're just like, "You're the DMC champion? Alright, cool. We'll have you here next week."

How do your parents and your friends respond to your success?

Well, I never had that many friends, so the couple of friends I have, they're straight. They go into every club free. They got it good in Miami. My mom, she's proud as hell. Every time I'm in a magazine, she's like,

"Hey, look at my son!" It's cool. My dad digs it. That's what I like about them. They were real supportive.

Let's talk about your style. Tell me about the dynamics that you use.

Dynamics are real important, because it controls the crowd a lot. You can do the easiest thing, but if you make it sound more in-your-face, people just freak out. I like bringing it down and then all of a sudden BAM! "Wow! What the hell was that?"

I like using a lot of different stuff, so people can just see a lot of movement. So, they can be like, "Whoa, he's moving a lot." The visual aspect is very, very important. That's half the show.

You seem to be really ambidextrous. You can scratch and manipulate the faders equally well with either hand. You're just moving around all the time. How did you develop that?

That's the "broke" style. My old mixer kept messing up. Every time it would break down, I would be too broke to buy a new fader. So when it would break on the right side, I'd just start cuttin' on the left side. If they were both like that, then I'd start cutting with the up-faders. That's how I learned, man.

Talk a little bit about your use of tape on the records.

Let's see, for the DMC, I don't like to have headphones on because it takes too much time to cue it up, so I just needle drop it on the tape, and BOOM, you're right there. You don't have to cue it up or nothin'. I use white tape right at the cut. I mark it so that it hits the needle when the music starts.

The other thing about your playing that knocks me out is the unique combinations that you do. How do you conceptualize that stuff?

Well, when I'm putting a routine together I'm just thinking of the sounds. I'm thinking of how I could use them for the transitions, and all that. I try not to do the same stuff or get too technical, that's why I do a lot of different stuff. I'm not the greatest scratcher or the greatest beat juggler or the best body-trick guy. But I have a little bit of everything. I try to be as on-point as I can be. I try not to lose the rhythm or nothin'.

Do you play any other instrument besides turntable?

I was in band in high school, I played marimba. I played anything on percussion.

Do you feel like that background helped you?

Oh, yeah. Hell, yeah. It helped me understand music better.

Where have you been at this point? Where have you played?

Pretty much everywhere. I've been in Japan, Australia. . . .

What were the crowds like in Japan?

They were really into it, man. Really, really into it. Right before I went on they had this whole huge intro for me on the big screen. I was like, "Damn!" It was crazy.

On a typical gig, how long would you play?

I play an hour and a half. I mix a lot, but I make it entertaining, so the turntablist kids don't leave. See, a lot of turntablist kids really don't go out to have fun, they're just there to see the turntablist. So I started mixing because I wanted to see the crowd move a little bit more and then kill 'em at the end. They go wild. That's always the catch. You spin all night and then at the end you hit 'em with the bomb.

Talk about spinning for a while. What's important there?

I think selection is important. Just having the right tunes. I won't play much commercial stuff, I'll just play what I like. More hip-hop stuff, instead of just what's on the radio.

How much of each record will you play?

I mix real quick. I just play one verse of every song, just to keep movin', and I'll play around with the tempo. I'll usually start slow with some old stuff and then pick up the pace.

Who are some of your favorite turntablists?

Q, Swamp, Roc Raida, Sinister.... Well, actually all of the X-men and all of the Pit Bulls, Jazzy Jeff, Cash Money, Scratch. But, I didn't even get to hear all those guys until I was older. I grew up in Miami, and that's a bass-oriented city, so I grew up with people like Magic Mike.

How long does it take you to put together a new battle routine?

For the first one, I wasn't really that booked or nothin', so I had time. I wouldn't practice every day, but I had time every other month to just work on it. This last year, I was stressed out because I was having a baby at the same time. And before that, I was on the road constantly, so I was never home. I was having anxiety attacks and breakdowns, and so I just took out one month. No bookings. I just stayed home and I came up with my routine in that one month.

How do you practice?

I used to have the equipment in my room. So if I was watching television, I would just practice on the commercial breaks, or if there was nothing on TV, I would just start scratchin'.

Where do you think turntablism is going? Where would you like to take it yourself?

I'd like to see it get more musical, because right now it's mostly technical stuff. Sometimes a crowd really doesn't get that. But if you had a band of DJs that had songs, like a regular band. You could do songs live, as well as do them on the records, and get more musical with it. That's where I see it going in the future, but it's still too electronic. It's still too techy and stuff.

In a year from now, where would you like to be career-wise?

I'd like to be the first third-year-in-a-row champion. I'm gonna take off two months before the DMC to practice. I've never done that, but I'm taking this one real serious.

Where would you like to be once your career has gone on for a while?

Well, I'd like to be making music. I'd like to have my own turntable band. It's more fun when you jam with other people. When you jam by yourself, it's cool, but when you jam with other people, you're trying to outshine everybody. There's that competitive-level thing going on.

That's great. So, what's your advice for young DJs?

Keep practicing. Keep doing what you're doing because that's how you get good. I don't think it's something you're born with. I think you're born with a good ear, but for any musical instrument, I think it's just practice and determination. Just keep practicing.

20. Kuttin Kandi

DJ as activist

Kuttin Kandi is a DJ, an activist, and a pioneer. Born and raised in Queens to Filipino parents, she is one of a growing number of female DJs.

How did you get started DJing?

I was always interested. My father was a DJ—not like a hip-hop DJ. He was more into the classics, like disco. He had early stages of hip-hop and early stages of rap when it started coming out. He showed me a couple of things on TV and things that were coming out in the '80s, when it started blowing up a lot bigger. I think it was Grand Master Flash. Sometimes there would be b-boys, like breakers, dancing. Also, he used to take me to the parks whenever kids danced, so I was around it a lot. My dad was very into music so he was open to anything. He wasn't a closed-minded parent.

I didn't really get into DJing until much later on, in high school. I was sixteen, but even then, I still didn't get serious. I couldn't afford my own turntables. At the time I was such a rebellious kid and I used to ask my dad, "Can you get me turntables?" He would be like, "No, you wouldn't be serious. Later on." I finally bought turntables when I was eighteen, an old 1200 from a friend, and then a new 1210. So I had both of those, but I actually didn't even have a mixer, yet.

How did you use two turntables without a mixer?

Oh my god, you don't know! I borrowed Roley's mixer, but it was already bleeding, so I really needed a mixer to learn everything. Before my father died, he was looking for his mixer and we couldn't find it anywhere. Then one summer we were cleaning out the attic, and in a box was my father's mixer. It was like a sign to me. It's like a 1970s mixer, in a wooden box, and it was hard to move and budge the faders. From that mixer, I learned how to scratch. Which is probably the craziest thing to ever do because that fader was so tough, but I was so determined and I really wanted to learn all the turntablism skills. I even learned how to do the "flare" on it—at the time, the flare was the hardest scratch, and it was brand new and everyone want to learn it.

How did you go about learning?

I was doing the party thing. DJing the parties. You know, not like the big clubs of New York City. I pretty much hit a lot of the Asian circuit. I was spinning at those scenes and being popular there. I would do a couple of other hip-hop parties, but I was still shy behind the turntables. I don't know why. I guess I wasn't confident of my skills yet. I was sixteen when I did my first party. I didn't do really well there. [Laughs]

Then later on, when I was about eighteen, I got a lot more confident and I started doing more and more parties. My confidence kept building, but I still felt like I needed more experience, so I started throwing my own parties. And my confidence started coming out and I was like, "Alright, I'm not gonna be shy behind the turntables anymore." That's when I got into the battles. I used to watch the guys, before 5th Platoon even started; I used to see them practice with the X-men, the X-ecution-ers. I wanted to learn so bad. I was so amazed by their skills and I wanted a part of it, but I remember back in the day when I first started DJing, no one really took me seriously. No one really believed that I really wanted to do it. They just said "Oh, she's just a girl and she just wants to learn because she thinks it's cute." [Laughs]

But I really was determined. I really wanted to learn. For a while, they were always practicing, and when I had my turntables, I would come home and try to do whatever they did. And I would never tell anyone that I was learning. Right after, I would see the X-ecutioners' perform-ance on stage, or the crew's performance on stage, I would go right home and practice. Everyone knew I DJ'd, but they didn't know I was learning. I knew I had to wait for the right moment, and I did. I waited almost two years before I did my first show.

What was the right moment?

The first Table Turns in '97, that was the first time I showed off my skills to everybody. And everybody was shocked. All the X-ecutioners were there and Apollo was there. Everyone was shocked.

So, you knew all these guys, but they didn't know that you'd been prac-ticing?

No, they didn't know I'd been practicing. [Laughs] It was a good feeling, though.

That's a great story. What are you doing these days, in terms of DJing?

Well, I DJ with 5th Platoon and I DJ with Anomalies—my all female hip-hop group. We have about sixteen females in the crew. We have four MCs. I'm the DJ. We have two beat girls. The seven of us are the main group, but the rest are artists and singers and all that. We're a really big hip-hop female group trying to show positive roles of women in hip-hop.

Sounds like a great project.

Yeah, it's one of my most important ones. Not that my other ones aren't, its just that there's not enough positive women in hip-hop right now. I'm the cofounder with my friend Helixx, she's one of the MCs. We used to go to all the hip-hop events together. There weren't a lot of women that would go, besides groupies. One day we were like, "Hey, you're an MC and I'm a DJ, and I have one of the beat girls. We should just get together."

So we formed our group, Anomalies, and we realized that we had the same mission, which was show that there are positive women in hip-hop with real talent. There are not enough women out there. There is Behamadia, there's Lauryn Hill, but there's just not enough. Usually in an industry, when they feel like they have one female, they don't feel like they need another. So, we put this together, our group, in '95 around the same time 5th Platoon started. I couldn't be down with 5th Platoon yet [laughs] so I was part of Anomalies. 5th Platoon, I had to pay my dues to be in there. I had to wait until '97. In April '97, I was put down in 5th Platoon.

Tell me about your history with 5th Platoon and how they got started.

5th Platoon got started with Roley Ro, Daddy Dog, and Neal Armstrong. The three of them got together and started practicing all the time. Then they started practicing with the X-ecutioners, the X-men at the time. We would go to Neal's house and he used to have basement DJ battles. We would all go there: us, The X-ecutioners, and I would just be the watch, the judge, actually. They used to put in dollars and whoever won the DJ battle would take the money.

It would be like Roley vs. Total Eclipse and Sinister vs. Daddy Dog. It would be a whole big battle in the basement. We would call it the Sparring Sessions at Neal's: the Neal Music Seminar, after the New Music Seminar.

Eventually, they met Doughboy and he started practicing with the crew. He was the hardcore scratcher. At the time, he was known as the best East-Coast scratcher, because he was the only one who had all the scratches from the West Coast that QBert was doing at the time. We've had several guests in the basement. There was Disc, Shortcut, Spinbad of the Cold Cuts Crew. Then they met Vin Rock again, another year later, and he was practicing with us, and then he was put down in our crew. I didn't get put down until a month after him, but I was with the guys since way back when they started.

I was considered part of the crew because I was their main supporter and I was their fan, but I wasn't really initiated into the group until . . . I had to prove myself. I had to win battles. I had to place. And I didn't start battling until '97.

What was the first battle that you ever entered?

The first battle that I was in was this radio DJ battle called the 105.9 DJ Battle. Shortcut was judging, Total Eclipse, Theodore, and I think it was Grand Master Kaz. It was me, Roley, Doughboy, and other DJs. It was a very interesting battle, pretty much the most original DJ battle I've been in, because in one of the rounds they give you these house records a week before the battle, then you have to come up with something with the house records. Everybody is given the same records, and they were really hard to come up with something on. I came up with something okay, pretty good. I actually got the highest score in that round. Roley ended up winning first and Doughboy got second and I got third. So, that was my first battle and I got third place. So that wasn't too bad.

What other battles have been significant in your career?

The '98 USA DMC Finals. I don't think any other female made it that far. I've been in over 20 battles from '97 to '98, so there are so many I can't remember. I was in ITF a couple times. I got second place regionals for the DMC in '98.

I'm the New York Source champion of '98. I battled Roley in that. Me and Roley went head to head against each other in the final round. The thing is, me and Roley don't really tell anyone that we're a couple. One of the people at the Source knew that we were. J Roo announced it on the microphone, and the whole crowd knew. "Oh, you're gonna lose to your girl. If you lose to your girl, that would be an embarrassment." He put Roley in a position where he felt uncomfortable.

It was crazy, and me and Roley went head to head, and I amazingly beat Roley. But if we had another round in that battle I know I would have lost. Roley's a really great person to go up against. I was lucky that night I won against him.

Did it affect your relationship at all?

Oh, no. Not at all. [Laughs] Roley's always one of the most modest people I know. He really is. He's always happy. He's one of my biggest supporters.

What do you see as being the future of DJing?

One of the biggest things that I push for is for more women to come into the DJ field, because it's the only way men will stop seeing us as "women DJs," "female DJs," or "girl DJs." They would just see us as DJs, period. No girl before it. No female before it. You know? We don't go around saying, "Oh look, she's a female doctor." It'll take some time, but I know it would happen eventually. I think right now there's a lot of misconceptions about being a female DJ. I know I feel it a lot of times, that I'm not allowed to make any mistakes, that I get more criticism than anyone else, or if I get a little spotlight, they'll automatically say, "Oh, she just got it because she's a female DJ." I've gotten used to it, but at the same time, I want it to end. The only way I think that can happen is if there are more women in this field.

What are your plans for the future?

I love music and music is my thing. I wanna take turntablism as far as I can and show everyone that this can be music. It's all music. Just as QBert has proved that to the world. I want to take it more into the realms of hip-hop again. You hear all the mainstream, and all the MTV and BET and all that stuff. They show DJing, but it's really just a gimmick. I want to show how the DJ can be a real producer through using the turntables. Plus, I want to get into production and be a producer. Not just in the hip-hop field, either. Get into r&b, or more like soul. Work with artists like Stevie Wonder or Aretha. Make an album one day.

I'm going to go back to school at St. John's here in New York to study education. For some reason, DJing has opened so many doors and made me see what else I wanted to do in this world. I've traveled and met people I wanted to work with, and started doing benefit shows as well as a lot of work with community and social issues. I've done workshops and lectures on hip-hop in high schools and universities. All these things made me realize I really want to be a teacher, I want to work with kids. I'm starting a program here in New York, a mentoring program for adults and for kids . . . a lot of the kids from the ghettos. I'm gonna start a hip-hop program and teach positive things and be a positive role model.

About the Author

Photo by Stacy Briscoe.

Stephen Webber is an Emmy-winning composer, record producer, and professor of music production and engineering at Berklee College of Music.

A DJ since the late '70s, Webber left his highly rated drive-time radio show to champion the music of Don Cherry, Herbie Hancock, and Miles Davis as the host of Infinite Jazz, while earning a degree in jazz guitar at the University of North Texas.

A scholarship student of Juilliard's Sharon Isbin at Aspen, Webber holds a master's degree in classical guitar performance with an emphasis in electronic composition.

As head of the guitar and music technology curriculums at Austin Peay State University, Webber founded the MIDI Committee, one of the first college-level electronic music ensembles.

Webber has produced and engineered 75 records and CDs, and composed the music for dozens of films and nationally broadcast television programs. Webber received an Emmy nomination for his score to the animated film *Zoetrobics*, which he recorded at Lucasfilm's Skywalker Ranch. He won an Emmy in '97 for music he wrote for PBS.

Webber studied writing at Harvard, and has published several articles in *Audio Media*, *ProSound News*, *Berklee Today*, *Electronic Musician*, and *Mix Magazine*.

Webber has taught record production and remixing at Berklee for several years, and is currently developing the first-ever curriculum at a major music college for the study of the turntable as a musical instrument.

Webber serves as a member of the Board of Overseers at the New England Conservatory.

Index